Who sold the first hamburgers?
The brothers, Maurice and Richard MacDonald set up business near Pasadena in 1940.

What is your Achilles' Heel?
Your weak spot! The Greek hero Achilles was dipped in the River Styx by his mother. This protected him from harm - except the heel by which she held him. One day he was killed by an arrow in his heel!

Does the colour red make a bull angry?
The bull is colour blind and does not see red at all. It charges the bullfighter's cape because it is waved in front of it, and this makes the bull mad!

What is a jumping bean?
Have you seen a Mexican bean jump? A tiny caterpillar, living inside the bean, moves around when it is warm. It changes into a moth and emerges from the bean through the hole it made as a caterpillar.

What is smoke?
The gases and unburned fuel that rise with the hot air from a fire. Smoke contains acids that harm plant life and corrode buildings.

Who played the pipes of Pan?
Pan was the Greek God of flocks and herds. He was half man and half goat and he had pointed ears, goat's horns and hooves. He played on a set of panpipes.

Who made the Tin Lizzie?
In 1908 Henry Ford, the American car manufacturer made a car for everybody. He made 15 million cars by mass production.

Why do men raise their hats?
In the Middle Ages knights would raise their visors to show they were friends not foes, and the tradition has continued as a gesture of politeness.

Is the Earth round?
It is almost spherical in shape. It bulges out a little at the equator and is slightly flatter at the poles.

Why was the Panama Canal built?
It enabled ships to take a short cut between the Atlantic and the Pacific, and avoid going around Cape Horn. The first ship passed through the 82km (51mile) long canal in 1914.

Was Cleopatra an Egyptian?
The Queen of Egypt was of Greek descent. She was almost certainly born in the city of Alexandria, which was a major Greek city in those days.

Who named New York?
At first the Dutch named it New Amsterdam. In 1664 the British took over the settlement and re-named it New York after the Duke of York, brother of Charles!

Who was Echo?
In Greek mythology the nymph Echo fell in love with Narcissus. Because he didn't return her love, she faded into just an answering voice.

What happened to Narcissus?
As a punishment, he fell in love with his own reflection. Like Echo, he pined away and was changed into the flower named Narcissus.

Who found the Victoria Falls?
David Livingstone the Scottish missionary and explorer. He traced the course of the Zambesi in Africa and discovered Lake Malawi and the Victoria Falls.

What flavour comes from an orchid?
The scented seed pods from certain kinds of orchid flavour sweet dishes and drinks with vanilla. The Aztecs used to flavour chocolate drinks with the pods.

Is the Pekinese from China?
The Chinese have bred these dogs for over 5,000 years. Only members of their royal family were allowed to own them. Five of these dogs were brought secretly to Europe in 1898.

Can you find the Moon in a window?
In 1969 rock from the Moon was brought back to Earth by Apollo astronauts. A tiny piece is sealed in a stained glass window in Washington Cathedral, USA.

Who built the Ark?
Noah was warned by God of a great flood. He built an ark big enough to take his family and two of every species of animal. When the flood was over the ark came to rest on Mount Ararat.

How old is Mickey Mouse?
This world famous mouse was first seen in the cartoon *Steam Boat Willie* in 1928. His creator Walt Disney used his own voice for the mouse.

Are elephants afraid of mice?
This is completely false. Mice are often found in elephants' cages in zoos and circuses. The two animals don't seem to notice each other at all.

How does an octopus move?
To propel itself through the water, it squirts water backwards from a tube under its head.

What is the Milky Way?
It is a galaxy of millions of stars that stretch in a milky white band across the sky at night.

Where are the Antipodes?
Places exactly opposite each other through the centre of the globe. To people living in Britain, the Antipodes are Australia and New Zealand.

What is liquorice?
It is made from the roots of the liquorice plant which is crushed and the juice extracted. When it solidifies, it is made into glossy black sticks to be used in sweets, drinks and medicines.

Who sings the Marseillaise?
It is the French national anthem composed in 1792. It was first sung in Paris at the time of the French Revolution.

When did the first crossword appear?
On December 21 1913 in the *New York World*. It was compiled by American journalist Arthur Wynne.

What was Eskimo-pie?
The name of the first choc-ice! It was invented by an American called C.K. Nelson in 1922 and given the name Eskimo-pie.

What was the guillotine?
A machine for cutting off the heads of all the people sentenced to death. Named after Dr Guillotin who suggested its use.

How much do you drink in your lifetime?
The average person drinks 50,000 litres (11,000 gallons) of liquid.

Does a pencil contain lead?
The lead in pencils is made from graphite which is a form of carbon found in layers between rock.

This edition published in 1994.

Published by
Grandreams Limited,
Jadwin House, 205/211 Kentish Town Road, London, NW52JU.

QA1

Printed in Czech Republic.

500 QUESTIONS AND ANSWERS

Written by Anne McKie, illustrated by Ken McKie

What is on Easter Island?

On a small isolated island in the south eastern Pacific are scattered about 1,000 giant statues. Some weigh up to 90 tonnes and are 9.5m (32ft) tall. No one really knows how the Polynesians carved or raised these statues.

What large animal was first discovered in 1900?

The okapi is a shy animal related to the giraffe. It lives in the dense rainforests of central Africa and eats a diet of leaves and shoots. It was completely unknown until 1900.

Is an iceberg salty?

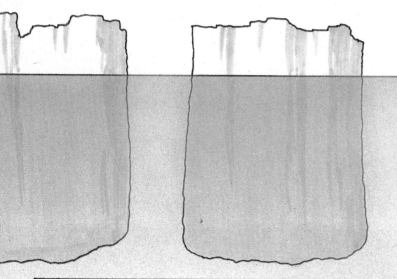

Found in the Arctic and Antarctic regions, icebergs are floating masses of ice that have broken away from a glacier. They float in the sea, carried by currents in the water and the wind. Gradually they are melted by the sun and the warm water into which they drift. They are not salty because they are made of snow!

Do bananas grow on trees?

They grow on tropical plants as tall as trees, up to 3m (10ft) high. The bananas grow on a single stalk, often 70-160 fruit in one bunch. The plant is cut down but grows back again next season.

Where do you find gargoyles?

Stonemasons in the Middle Ages carved animal heads, devils and grotesque faces as water spouts. They took rainwater from church or cathedral roofs and kept the water clear of the stone walls.

What is a mummy?

A dead body that has been embalmed or preserved and sometimes wrapped in hundreds of metres of bandages. The name mummy comes from the Persian word 'mummia', which means 'tar'. Because the bodies were black with age, people wrongly believed they had been soaked in tar.

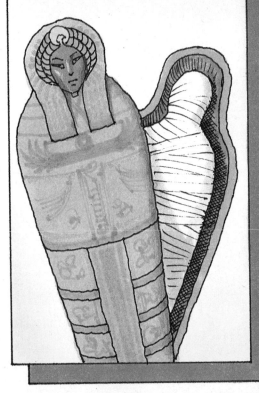

Who was Hannibal and how did he cross the Alps?

He was the leader of the Carthaginian army who invaded Italy in 218 BC. He took an army of 40,000 men and 37 elephants over the Pyrenees and the Alps from Spain to Italy. Hannibal floated his elephants across rivers on huge rafts - but he never conquered Rome!

What is perspective?

To draw solid objects you give the impression of distance or depth by making parallel lines converge to a vanishing point at eye level or on the horizon.

What are stalactites and stalagmites?

Stalactites are formed in limestone caves by the constant dripping of water from the roof. Limestone deposits cause shapes like icicles to form from the ceiling of caves. Water drips from them onto the floor and a stalagmite is produced. After thousands of years the two may grow together to make a solid pillar.

Is a sponge a plant or an animal?

A sponge is one of the simplest forms of animal life. It feeds by drawing in water through its pores and extracting food. We use the dead skeleton of a sponge to wash with in the bath!

Where does a female puffin lay her eggs?

Although puffins spend most of their time far out at sea, they also rest on rocks and cliffs in large colonies.

These birds dig long burrows in the ground using their beaks and feet. Their eggs are laid in a little nesting chamber at the end of the underground burrow.

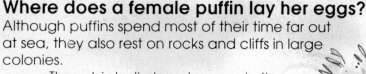

Who lives at Number Ten?

The official residence of British Prime Ministers is number 10 Downing Street. It is in a side-street off Whitehall, near the Houses of Parliament.

It was built by Sir George Downing in 1680, and in 1738 George II offered it to Sir Robert Walpole, who was Britain's first Prime Minister.

Next door, at number 11, lives the Chancellor of the Exchequer.

How can you draw an ellipse?

To draw a perfect oval or ellipse, stick two pins through a paper covered board. Join them with a thread that is longer than the distance between the pins. Put a pencil in the thread, keep it tight and draw an ellipse.

What is a Möbius strip?

To make a Möbius strip, take a strip of paper, give it half a twist, then join the ends to form a band. Run a pencil round and you'll find the strip has one single edge. It was named after the 19th century mathematician Augustus Möbius.

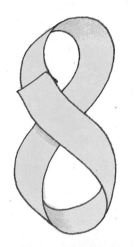

Who lives at the White House?

It is the official residence of the President of the United States of America. It is in Washington, the capital.

The White House was designed by an Irish architect and the foundation stone was laid in 1792. President John Adams was its first occupant in 1880.

The house was originally built of grey Virginian sandstone, but in August 1814 it was burned by British troops. After the war it was painted white to hide the marks made by the smoke.

Why do flowers smell?

To humans some flowers smell sweet and others smell disgusting. Certain flowers, that have an odour of decay are pollinated by flies and sometimes bats.

Some insects visit scented flowers to feed on pollen and sweet smelling nectar. As insects go from flower to flower they spread pollen, which in turn helps to make the seeds for next season's plants.

Who found the Dead Sea Scrolls?

One day in 1947, a Bedouin boy was looking for a lost goat along the cliffs by the Dead Sea. He threw a stone into the mouth of some caves and heard the sound of breaking pottery.

Once inside he discovered several clay jars containing decayed parchment scrolls, on which were written Bible stories over 2,000 years old. These and many other manuscripts found in caves nearby, became known as the Dead Sea Scrolls - one of the most important discoveries of all time!

Who was Johnny Appleseed?

His real name was John Chapman. All his life he roamed Ohio Territory planting apple seeds and trees. He walked barefoot, even in winter. His clothes were ragged, he wore an upturned pot on his head and carried a Bible in his shirt.

What is the most poisonous creature in the sea?

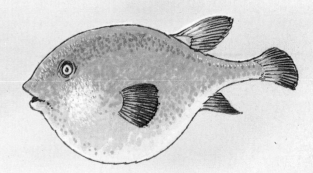

The puffer fish, which puffs itself up when threatened, is one of the world's most poisonous fish. They are eaten in Japan, after careful preparation by a trained chef, who removes the poisonous sac.

This delicacy is known as a fugu and is eaten raw. Many people die each year from eating this dish. The poison paralyses the nervous system and there is no known antidote.

Which famous storyteller was a cobbler's son?

Hans Christian Andersen was born in Odense, Denmark. He was the son of a poor sick cobbler, who died when Hans was eleven.

At the age of fourteen he went to Copenhagen to become an actor or singer, but everyone laughed at him. For a time he walked the streets, hungry, lonely and friendless.

In the years to come he tried all kinds of writing, but without success. At last a play of his was performed at the Royal Theatre, and when his first book of fairy tales was published four years later, he became famous overnight.

He will always be remembered for such well known stories as *The Ugly Duckling, The Snow Queen, The Emperor's New Clothes, The Tinderbox* and many more.

Where is the statue of the Little Mermaid?

Sitting on a rock in Copenhagen harbour is a bronze statue of the Little Mermaid. She is the heroine of one of Hans Christian Andersen's best known fairy tales.

Who were the brothers Grimm?

The brothers Jacob and Wilhelm, two language professors, collected old folk tales told in Germany. They published them as a collection of fairy tales. *Snow White, Hansel and Gretel, Rumpelstiltskin* and *Rapunzel* were just a few.

Who wrote *Cinderella*?

Red Riding Hood, Puss in Boots, Sleeping Beauty and *Cinderella* were all written in France by Charles Perrault in the 18th-century.

Who was Scheherazade?

The stories in the *Arabian Nights* were told by Scheherazade to her husband the King. He always killed his wives the day after they were married.

Scheherazade did not die, because every night she told him a different story and stopped at the most exciting part. Each morning the King spared her life and waited to hear that night how the story ended.

Some of the stories she told were *The Seven Voyages of Sinbad* and *Aladdin*.

Who translated these stories into English?

Sir Richard Burton the Victorian explorer, who together with Captain John Speke, led expeditions across East Africa to discover the source of the River Nile. As an old man he translated the *Arabian Nights*.

Who was Lewis Carroll?

His real name was Charles Lutwidge Dodgson, and he was a lecturer in mathematics at Oxford. Lewis Carroll was better known as the author of *Alice in Wonderland*. The story was told to his friends' children - one of whom was a nine-year-old girl called Alice.

Who was the boy who wouldn't grow up?

On December 27th 1904, a new play for children opened in London. It was J.M. Barrie's *Peter Pan*, the boy from Never Never Land who wouldn't grow up, together with Wendy, the Lost Boys and the evil Captain Hook. It became the most famous play ever written for children.

How did Mark Twain get his name?

The American writer's real name was Samuel L. Clemens. For a time he worked on a Mississippi steamboat as a river pilot. The boatmen shouted 'mark twain' (second mark) as they measured the shallow water to a depth of two fathoms (3.6m or 12 ft).

Best known of his humorous books are *The Adventures of Tom Sawyer* and *The Adventures of Huckleberry Finn*.

Which writer was the Secretary of the Bank of England?

Kenneth Graham who wrote *The Wind in the Willows* was a banker. His stories of Mole, Rat, Toad and Badger were first published in 1908.

Who wrote the *Just So* stories?

Rudyard Kipling was born in India and wrote many stories about the animals and people there. His *Jungle Book* tells of an Indian boy Mowgli, who was brought up with wolves. In the tale he becomes friendly with the animals and helps them overcome their enemies. In the *Just So* stories, Kipling tells how the leopard got its spots, the elephant its trunk, and the camel its hump!

Was Sherlock Holmes a real detective?

No, he was not a real person, but he was probably the most famous fictional detective of all time!

In 60 stories written by Edinburgh doctor Sir Arthur Conan Doyle, Sherlock Holmes and his friend Dr Watson lived in London at 221B Baker Street. Amazing powers of observation and deduction helped Holmes solve the most bizarre of crimes.

When did we domesticate animals?

The earliest animals to live together with humans were goats, sheep, cattle, pigs and dogs.

Stone Age people had wolf-like dogs around their camps over 10,000 years ago, and may have hunted with them. Goats and sheep were first domesticated in the Middle East, and provided early human beings with milk, wool and skins around 8,000BC.

Rabbits first lived with us as recently as AD1,000.

What are hieroglyphics?

They are a system of picture writing used by the ancient Egyptian priests. At first, pictorial symbols represented words that were easily recognised like man, bird, flower, Sun and eye. Later, as hieroglyphics developed, some symbols were used to represent sounds.

Modern scholars could not understand this writing until the early 1800s.

How was the mystery of hieroglyphics solved?

The puzzle of this strange writing was solved in 1799 when a large black stone was discovered near Rosetta in Egypt.

It told the same story repeated in hieroglyphics, ancient Greek and demotic. It was finally deciphered in 1822 by Jean Champollion when the riddle of the Rosetta Stone was solved.

What was Archimedes' great discovery in the bath?

Archimedes was a great mathematician and scientist born in 287 BC. He is mostly remembered for discovering a fact that became known as 'Archimedes' Principle'. All bodies weighed when immersed in fluid, show a loss of weight equal to the fluid they displace.

Archimedes made this startling discovery while he was in his bath. He was so excited that he rushed out in the street naked shouting "Eureka!" This is Greek for "I have found it!"

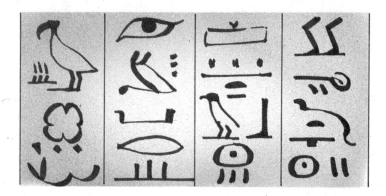

Who planted the first apple trees in Australia?

The ship The Bounty was commanded by Captain Bligh. In 1787 some of the crew, led by Fletcher Christian, mutinied against Bligh's cruel discipline and set him and 18 sailors adrift in a small boat.

This tiny boat crossed 5,793km (3,600 miles) of open sea and landed safely in the East Indies.

In 1805 Bligh was made governor of New South Wales and he planted Australia's first apple trees.

How long would it take to boil an ostrich egg?

To soft boil a hen's egg for breakfast would take four minutes. An ostrich's egg, the biggest bird's egg of all, would take at least 40 minutes to boil.

Where does chocolate come from?

The main ingredient of chocolate is cocoa from the fruit of the cacao tree. The fruit is the size of a small melon and contains around 40 beans that are dried, roasted, then ground into a fine powder.

The Aztecs drank an unsweetened chocolate drink, often mixed with wine and flavoured with pimento and pepper.

In the mid-nineteenth century solid chocolate bars were made in Europe from cocoa powder, cocoa butter, sugar and sometimes milk.

What happened to the American buffalo?

The American buffalo is really a bison. Millions of them roamed across the plains of North America before the arrival of white people.

The Indians hunted them for food, clothes, tepees - even some of their boats were covered in buffalo hide - but their numbers remained the same.

During the 1800s they were hunted almost to extinction, to help feed the thousands of men employed in building the new railroads and for their cheap hides. In 1889 their numbers had dropped from 20,000,000 to just over 1,000. Luckily the remaining herds are now protected.

What is a monolith?

Ayers Rock in the desert plains of central Australia is one of the world's largest monoliths, which means an upright single stone. It is 348m (1,143ft) high and nearly 9km (6 miles) round.

This eroded sandstone mountain is a sacred place to the Australian Aborigines - in the large caves at the base of the rock, the walls are decorated with their early paintings.

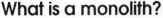

Is the koala a bear?

Although koalas look like small bears, they are related to the ring-tailed possum and the great glider, and are not bears at all!

They spend between 18 and 20 hours a day resting, and four to six hours munching the leaves of eucalyptus trees.

What is a laughing jackass?

A type of kingfisher called the kookaburra has a call that sounds like loud, hysterical laughter. These birds live in the grasslands of Australia, often near water. They hunt snakes, mice and insects.

Why do camels have big feet?

Camels are specially adapted for travelling across the desert. They do not sink into the sand because their feet have broad soles that cover a large area, so the pressure on the sand is low.

Who first brought tobacco to England?

Sir Walter Raleigh introduced pipe-smoking into court circles in 1586. He was a great favourite with Queen Elizabeth I. Unfortunately, after her death he fell out of favour. He was imprisoned for 12 years and then beheaded.

Why are the eggs of some birds pointed?

A pointed egg will roll round in a circle! The eggs of certain sea birds are this shape so they do not roll off the cliff edges where the birds breed.

Why does a peacock display his feathers?

The peacock is the male bird, the female peahen has plain brown feathers and a small tail. The peacock spreads his brilliant fan-like tail to attract the female.

What is an angler fish?

This saltwater fish has a thin spine that grows from its head - just like a fishing rod! On the end is a growth that looks like a piece of bait. This attracts smaller fish, which the angler quickly gobbles up.

Who really invented the telephone?

Alexander Graham Bell and Elisha Gray both filed applications for the patent on the very same day in New York, January 14 1876. Bell arrived at the Patent Office at 12.00 noon, Gray at 2.00pm.

After a long court case, judges decided that Bell invented the telephone.

How can you tell the age of a tree?

Each year as the tree grows it adds a new ring of sap wood beneath the bark. If the tree is cut down, you can estimate its age by counting the rings on a cross-section of the trunk.

Which was the last planet to be discovered?

The ninth planet, Pluto, was discovered by a young American astronomer, Clyde Tombaugh, in 1930. Pluto is 5,970 million km (3,700 million miles) from the Sun and has one moon.

What was a quagga?

A type of wild horse with stripes like a zebra. Vast herds once roamed the plains of South Africa. It was hunted for its skin and became extinct. The last quagga was seen in 1875.

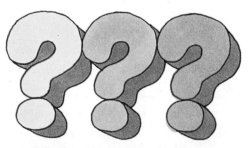

Why do sailors sleep in hammocks?

Until the hammock was invented, sailors simply slept on the wooden decks.

On one of his voyages to the West Indies, Sir John Hawkins came across some of the natives sleeping in hanging beds slung from two trees. They called them 'hammacoes'. So, from 1586 on, all sailors on Sir John's ships slept in hammocks - and the habit spread to seafarers all over the world.

Who fought in a tournament?

In the Middle Ages, knights on horseback fought one another in mock battles or tournaments for sport and entertainment.

Jousting took place in the tilting-yard in a special enclosure surrounded by stands for spectators. Two knights in full armour would charge at each other on either side of a wooden barrier, each one trying to unseat the other. Although they carried blunt lances, injuries were common.

The tournaments were really a chance for knights to practise ready for real battles or war.

Who was King Canute?

He was the son of the King of Denmark and he ruled England from 1016-1035.

When his courtiers became too flattering, saying he was all powerful and could do anything, King Canute decided to prove them wrong!

He had his throne placed on the beach in front of the incoming tide. As the water lapped around his feet, he ordered the waves to stop and the tide to go back. Of course it did not! This way the wise King showed he had the powers of a man and not a god.

Where is Table Mountain?

Cape Town, South Africa, lies at the foot of Table Mountain. This majestic flat-topped mountain sometimes has a flat white cloud covering the top, that looks just like a tablecloth!

What is the Pentagon?

A huge five-sided building in Alexandria, Virginia, across the Potomac River from Washington DC. It houses the US Defence Department's offices for the army, navy, air force and coastguard.

You could fit eighty-three soccer pitches into the 604,000 sq. m (6,500,000 sq. ft) floor area, and spend all day running up and down the 28 km (17.5 miles) of corridors.

Who has been surfing for centuries?

Although the sport of surfing reached California around 1900, it was seen much earlier by Captain Cook in 1778, when he arrived in Hawaii.

The sport probably came to Hawaii when the Tahitians migrated there over 1,000 years earlier.

Which is the red planet?

In the reflected light of the Sun, the planet Mars shines red. The surface is made up of dry plains, mountains and craters. The redness is caused by the dust and oxidation of the rocks.

Who made the first sandwich?

John Montagu, the fourth Earl of Sandwich, is said to have invented the sandwich in 1762.

The Earl loved to gamble, and so as not to interrupt his card game a servant was ordered to bring him a piece of meat between two slices of buttered bread. That is how the Earl gave his name to the sandwich!

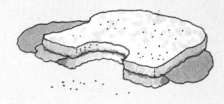

Which famous dog was rescued from a battle-field?

During the First World War, a tiny puppy trembling with shock was rescued from a German trench by an American soldier, Captain Lee Duncan.

The soldier took the puppy back to America, trained him and taught him tricks. The dog was called Rin Tin Tin, the German shepherd who became the most popular animal film star in the world!

What was a crinoline?

A hooped petticoat that was fashionable in the middle of the 19th century. The billowing skirts of Victorian times were held in place by a steel or whale-boned frame called a crinoline, which hung from the waist. It made the wearer's skirt look like a huge bell.

Underneath their crinolines, women wore several lacy petticoats and a pair of long pantaloons - just in case a strong wind blew!

Crinolines became so wide that women wearing them could not squeeze through a door or walk down the stairs - even sitting on a chair was difficult!

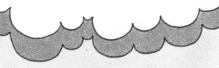

Was Julius Caesar a Roman Emperor?

Julius Caesar (102-44BC) was a Roman statesman and a general who conquered Gaul (now France and Belgium), and invaded Britain in 55BC.

He became the sole ruler and dictator of the Roman Empire, but was never the emperor.

He was stabbed to death in the Senate House by enemies who believed that he had too much power.

Who was Aesop?

He is thought to have been a slave who lived in Asia Minor in the 6th century BC.

He is remembered for the stories that he wrote and collected.

Which birds have the most beautiful feathers?

Birds of paradise from northern Australia and New Guinea are among the most colourful birds in the world.

To attract a mate, some birds show off their amazing plumage by hanging upside-down like an acrobat and spreading their tail feathers out.

Who hunts them?

The tribesmen of New Guinea make head-dresses from the beautiful feathers of these birds. They even wear the long tail feathers through their noses.

What were his stories called?

His stories were called fables; short tales with a moral. Aesop's fables had animal characters such as the tortoise and the hare:

A hare once challenged a tortoise to a race. The hare knew he was quicker than the tortoise so he rested on the way. The slow tortoise took his time, but he won the race. The hare was so confident that he had fallen asleep!

What is cork?

It is the outer bark of the cork oak tree, which grows in large numbers in Spain and Portugal. When a tree is 20-years-old the bark is cut and peeled off in rectangular pieces. This is repeated every 10 years, but it does not harm the tree. Cork is very light and floats on water.

Where would you find a tuatara?

The tuatara is a reptile found only in parts of New Zealand. It belongs to the stegosaurus family and has remained unchanged for over 200 million years. It is our only living contact with the dinosaurs.

The stegosaurus hunts at night, but don't worry - it's only about 75cm (30in) long!

Is the umbrella a modern invention?

The pharaoahs of ancient Egypt sat under ceremonial 'brollies' held by slaves. The Chinese used them before 1,000BC, but only royalty or court officials. Some looked like pagodas, four umbrellas high. King Louis XIII of France owned the first waterproof umbrella in 1637.

At the battle of Waterloo, English officers on

horseback held an umbrella in one hand and a sabre in the other. The Duke of Wellington's umbrella was made of oiled cotton with a concealed sword inside!

What did the Duke of Wellington give his name to?

During his campaigns in Belgium and Spain, the first Duke of Wellington got his feet muddy so he had a special pair of waterproof boots designed that reached as far as the knee - Wellingtons!

What happened to Pompeii?

Pompeii was a fashionable Roman town in the bay of Naples at the foot of Mount Vesuvius. On the morning of August 24th in the year AD79, there was a great crash, the ground shook and the sky went dark. The volcano Vesuvius had erupted so violently and suddenly that within a few hours the town of Pompeii was buried under layers of pumice and volcanic ash which rained down from above.

Many people were able to run from the city, but about 2,000 died, covered with a blanket of ash about three metres (10ft) deep. Four other nearby towns disappeared in the eruption including Herculaneum.

For hundreds of years the towns were forgotten, until in 1710 a peasant digging deep for a well found pieces of marble that were from Herculaneum.

Then in 1748 the town of Pompeii was discovered, but the main excavations did not begin on a large scale until 1860.

Digging revealed rows of shops, hundreds of homes, theatres, public baths and a huge amphitheatre. Even the food that had been left ready on the tables for lunch that day in AD 79 (bread, fruit, walnuts, sausages and eggs) had been preserved by the volcanic ash. Plaster casts have been made of the people and animals that lived and died there.

You can visit the ruins of Pompeii today and see what life was really like in Roman times, almost two thousand years ago.

What is pumice stone?

A very light and porous rock that floats in water. Pumice stone is found in volcanic areas.

It is formed by the quick cooling of molten volcanic lava as it pours out of the volcano. Air bubbles are trapped inside the rock from the foaming white hot lava. When the stone solidifies, gases inside are released and form tiny air pockets making the pumice stone feel very light.

Which is the world's smallest independent state?

It is the Vatican City in Italy, which has been the residence of the popes since the fifth century AD. It has a population of around 1,000, and no one is ever born there! The Vatican is the government centre of the Roman Catholic Church.

It lies within the boundaries of Rome, and covers an area of just 0.44 sq. m (0.17 sq. miles).

This tiny state has its own guards, money, flag, post-office, railway station, bank and daily newspaper. It also has a broadcasting station and telephone system. There's even an astronomical observatory!

Early in the 16th century, Pope Julius II asked Michaelangelo to design a uniform for the papal guard in the Vatican City. At the time there were 6,000 men in this army, all recruited from Switzerland. Nowadays there are only about 100 Swiss guards, but their uniform is exactly the same as that designed by Michaelangelo in the 1500s.

Millions of people visit the Vatican every year. Most of them come to see the Basilica of St Peters with its magnificent frescoes of biblical scenes painted on the ceiling of the Sistine Chapel.

What are frescoes?

They are paintings done in watercolour on walls or ceilings while the plaster is still wet. The painting must be finished before the plaster dries. The colours sink into the plaster and remain fresh and bright, often for hundreds of years.

Who was Michaelangelo?

He was an Italian painter, sculptor and architect who designed the great dome of St Peters. He is best known for his sculpture and his paintings in the Sistine Chapel. To reach the ceiling, Michaelangelo had to work on a scaffold lying flat on his back, often working long hours by candlelight.

The whole masterpiece took four years. During that time Michaelangelo painted 340 figures and covered 10,000 square feet of ceiling!

Who was Mother Goose?

No one knows who Mother Goose was, but her tales and rhymes have been told for centuries.

In 1696 some were written down by a French man Charles Perrault. Then they were published in Paris as a book containing eight stories.

Mother Goose tales were first translated into English in 1729. Then in 1785 some of our best loved nursery rhymes appeared in books in America.

What was a penny farthing?

This early bicycle got its name from the wheels, which resembled two English coins of the time, the large penny and the small farthing.

It was invented in 1871 in Coventry, England, by James Starley. For every turn of the pedals, a gear turned the big front wheel twice!

Did Lord Nelson ever suffer from sea sickness?

Lord Horatio Nelson, the most famous of all English admirals, joined the navy at the age of 12, but suffered from sea sickness all his life. He was killed during the Battle of Trafalgar in 1805.

Why does the Tower of Pisa lean?

Pisa is a town in northern Italy famous for its leaning tower, a campanile (bell tower) built for the cathedral and designed to carry the sound of bells as far as possible.

The white marble tower is 54.5m (179ft) high and weighs 14,150 tonnes. It leans because the foundations are not strong enough, just 3m (10ft) deep.

The building was started in 1173 and began to lean almost immediately. It took 200 years to complete, and the tower has tilted more over the years. The top is now 5.6m (18ft) out of true.

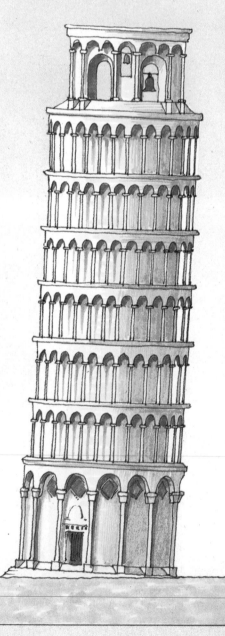

Who were the first people to climb Mount Everest?

The highest mountain in the world above sea level is Mount Everest in the Himalayas. It is 8,849m (29,030ft) high, although the depth of ice on the peak changes this a little.

It was first climbed in 1953 by Sir Edmund Hillary and the Sherpa, Tensing Norgay. They planted the flags of Britain, Nepal, India and the U.N. on the top.

Was Robinson Crusoe a real person?

Daniel Defoe's novel *Robinson Crusoe*, published in 1719, was based on the true story of a Scottish sailor Alexander Selkirk. After a quarrel at sea, he was left, at his own request, on the island of Juan Fernandez, Chile. He was rescued four years later.

Do ostriches really bury their heads in the sand?

No, when danger threatens, an ostrich may run away, often at 80.5km (50 miles) an hour. But it can also inflict terrible wounds by kicking out with its powerful legs and sharp toes.

What was the wooden horse of Troy?

This story is told in Homer's poem, the *Iliad*. Troy in Asia Minor, had been under siege by the Greeks for 10 years. The Greeks tricked the Trojans into opening the city gates for a great wooden horse, which was full of soldiers hidden inside. Once the gates were opened the Greek army followed and captured Troy.

What is a tornado?

A violent and destructive column of spinning air. A whirlwind with a wind speed at its centre that can reach 640kmh (400mph). This swirling funnel shaped cloud travels forward at about 65kmh (40mph) causing terrible destruction.

Do you know what cotton is?

Cotton grows on low bushes in the south eastern states of the USA, Egypt, Brazil and India. It is the fluffy tufts of white fibre (bolls) that grow round the cotton seeds.

Cotton is picked, and after cleaning it is spun into thread that can be woven into cloth.

How do you charm a snake?

Snakes cannot hear the music played to them by a snake charmer because they are deaf!

They copy the movements of the snake charmer and his flute - swinging from side to side as if they are hypnotised.

What did Laslo Biro invent?

In 1938 he invented the ballpoint pen. He was a Hungarian journalist and realised that the quick-drying ink he had seen used by the printing trade could be adapted for use in a pen.

What is a flying boat?

It is an aircraft that can land and take off from water. The underside of the plane is shaped like a boat. Each wing has a float underneath to keep the plane balanced in the water. Some, called amphibians, have wheels and can be used on land or on water.

What is different about the mule?

It is a hybrid animal with a donkey for a father and a horse for a mother. It has the strength of a horse, and is as hardy and as sure-footed as a donkey.

They are mainly used as pack animals, especially on rough roads. Mules can be quite stubborn at times!

Why is the sky blue?

The sky has no colour of its own. When sunlight (made up of all colours) passes through the atmosphere it is scattered around by millions of particles in the air.

The blue in the sunlight is scattered more than the other colours, so the sky appears to be blue.

Did cavemen ever hunt dinosaurs?

Dinosaurs have been extinct for more than 60 million years. Humans appeared on Earth two to four million years ago. The two have only met in stories and cartoons, or in films and television.

Do whales spout water?

Whales are mammals and must return to the surface of the water to breathe air. The whale's spout is its exhaled breath from a hole on the top of its head.

Whales are really spouting air, not water at all!

Where does sand come from?

Sand is made up of lots of bits of mineral substances, mostly silica or quartz. It is formed by the breaking down and weathering of rocks.

On the seashore, sand often contains minute particles of shell.

Did you know there are plants that eat insects?

The Venus flytrap closes, traps, then digests any insect that lands on its hair-covered leaves.

The pitcher plant captures insects that venture over the rim then fall to the bottom. A few plants grow large enough to trap small reptiles and animals. Some pitcher plants can open their lids and let rainwater in to drown their prey.

Venus flytrap

Pitcher plants

What is the world's largest and smelliest flower?

The rafflesia plant is the largest and smelliest! Up to 90cm (3ft) across, and weighing 7kg (15lb).

What is an abacus?

It is an ancient calculating machine, dating 5,000 years, that is still in use today.

Rows of beads threaded on wire represent units, tens, hundreds etc. To calculate, the beads are moved up and down or sideways.

ones

tens

hundreds

thousands

The beads show the number 3065

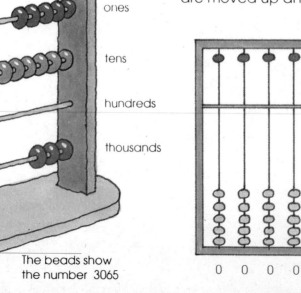

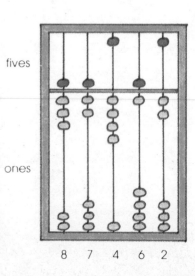

fives

ones

0 0 0 0 0 0   8 7 4 6 2

Did you know there are two types of camel?

The Bactrian camel from central Asia has two humps. The Arabian camel bred in S.E. Asia has one. The Arabian is taller and faster, and when bred for racing is known as a dromedary. The Bactrian is much sturdier and can carry heavy loads.

Do they store water in their humps?
A camel can extract some water from the food reserve of fat in the hump. It does not need to sweat to keep cool until its body temperature reaches 46°C (115°F).

Arabian Camel   Bactrian Camel

What is an optical illusion?
It occurs when the brain misunderstands something seen by the eyes. Study these pictures and you may be deceived by your own eyes.

What is a mirage?
An optical illusion caused by light rays bending in heat or cold. An object over the horizon can be seen in the sky.

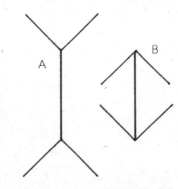

Are these two black faces or one white candlestick?

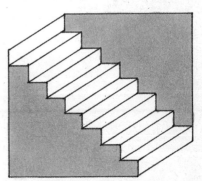

Is this flight of steps seen from above or below?

Is line A longer than line B?

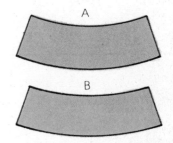

Is the top shape A bigger than the bottom shape B?

How wild was the West?

When the United States gained independence in 1783, only the eastern side of the country, up to the Mississippi River was explored. Soon daring men such as trappers, adventurers and gold miners began spreading west. The only law they recognised was the law of the gun!

What were wagon trains?

Rumours began to reach the eastern states of the great rich lands of the West. Stories of great rivers, plentiful supplies of food and gold made families decide to risk everything. They sold their homes and packed everything into a small covered wagon.

Because of the risk from Indians and robbers they travelled in large numbers called wagon trains.

Who were the mountain men?

These were the tough men who blazed the trails across America. Bearded and dressed in skins they were mainly beaver trappers. Because of their knowledge of the country, many became guides for the wagon trains.

How do you get gold from a river?

Small pieces of gold get washed down the rivers and collect in quiet pools. People would scoop up the sand from the river and swirl it around in a shallow pan. The heavier pieces of gold would be left at the bottom.

What was the pony express?

This was a way of carrying mail and news almost 3,200km (2,000 miles) across America. Riders would race at top speed for up to 32km (20 miles) then change horses and race on again. When they were exhausted another rider would take over. This famous service lasted less than two years before the telegraph took over.

Who were the cowboys?

As the population of the United States grew and settled into towns, cattle were needed to feed the people. Huge herds of half-wild longhorn cattle had to be looked after, rounded up and taken long distances to the railroad stations. This was the job of the cowboy.

Did cowboys carry guns?

Cowboys faced many dangers. Indians and cattle-rustlers would try to steal the herd, and animals such as bears, wolves and mountain lions preyed on the cattle and the cowboys. So every man would carry a revolver and a rifle.

What is a lariat?

It is a cowboy's rope. When a cow needed to be picked out from the herd, the cowboy would throw his rope over its head and quickly tie the other end to the saddle horn. The lariat would be about 10m (32ft) in length.

What are chaps?

The name comes from the Mexican word 'chaparejos'. They are heavy leather leg protectors.

   If the cowboy had to chase cattle into rough bush country his legs would get badly cut. Chaps also protected him from the horns of the cattle.

What is a cowboy's hat called?

The large wide-brimmed hats were nicknamed ten gallon hats. The proper name was a stetson, after the hat maker who designed them.

What is cattle branding?

Because the cattle roamed freely over large areas of land, the owners had to mark their own animals. They did this by burning a design into the hide. The cattle had very tough hide so this did not hurt.

Were there really outlaws?

Because of the huge size of the American West, and the small number of law officers, it was easy for criminals to avoid capture.

   Famous characters included Butch Cassidy and the Sundance Kid, and the woman cattle rustler, Belle Starr.

Butch Cassidy The Sundance Kid

Who was Davy Crockett?

He was a hunter and a politician. Texas once belonged to Mexico, but the American rulers fought against the Mexican ruler Santa Anna. Davy Crockett died at the battle of the Alamo.

What was the iron horse?

It was the name the Indians gave to the train. The railroad began to spread across America after the civil war ended in 1865. The Indians hated the railroad because it crossed their hunting ground.

Did you know the Union Jack was really three flags in one?

The English red cross of St George was combined with the Scottish flag of St Andrew in 1606. The Irish flag of St Patrick was included in 1800. Union Jack is the name given to the flag after the three flags were unified.

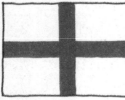
St George

St Andrew

St Patrick

What do the stars and stripes mean?

The flag of the United States of America is also nicknamed 'the stars and stripes'. The 13 stripes represent the 13 states that declared their independence in 1776. As new states joined the union, the flag changed 26 times. The 50 white stars represent the number of states in the whole of the union. The USA's anthem is the Star Spangled Banner.

Did unicorns ever exist?

The unicorn was a mythical beast that for centuries was believed to exist. The horse with a single horn in the middle of its head was used on coats of arms. Even today it is still a popular design symbol.

In the past people finding the long spiralled tusk of the narwal (sea unicorn) might have thought it belonged to a unicorn.

What are decibels?

A decibel (db) is a unit for measuring the loudness or intensity of sound. Whispering is 20db, speaking is 60db. The scale increases in units - a sound measured at 50db is ten decibels louder than one of 40db.

Long exposure to sounds of over 120db (a disco or rock concert) can damage hearing.

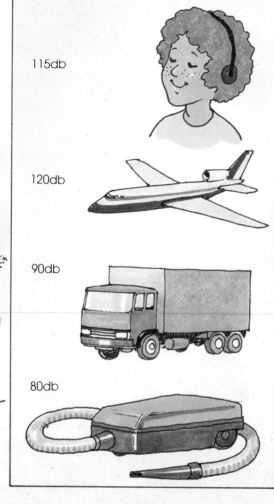

115db

120db

90db

80db

What bird is called a bone-breaker?

The lammergeier vulture or bone-breaker has a unique way of getting at its food. It drops bones from a height down onto a rocky surface, then flys down to eat the bone marrow. Vultures often drop eggs, shellfish and sometimes tortoises in the same way.

Who invented the zip fastener?

The zip fastener or zipper with small interlocking teeth was invented back in 1890 by American Whitecomb Judson. It took about 20 years before his invention was satisfactory. The zip was first used on snow boots.

What is an airship?

An airship is a sausage-shaped balloon filled with a lighter-than-air gas that makes it float. The early airships could carry passengers across the Atlantic, but they were slow and dangerous because they were filled with hydrogen gas which burns easily. Modern airships are filled with safe helium gas, but they are still slow.

When was food first put in cans?

Food in tin cans was first produced in Britain in 1812 by Donkin and Hall of London. They canned beef, mutton, vegetable stew, soups and carrots. These goods were very useful to the explorers of the day.

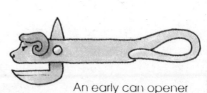

An early can opener

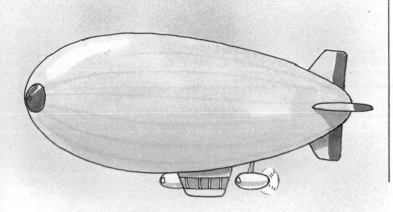

Can you stay warm in an igloo?

You can. The Eskimo igloo is a temporary home used on hunting trips. It is built by cutting large blocks of hard packed snow and placing them one on top of another to form a dome shaped house. Fur rugs are spread on the floor. Light and warmth come from a small lamp that burns seal oil.

What were mammoths?

They were hairy elephant-like mammals that stood 4.5m (14ft 9in) high. They lived in herds and roamed across northern Europe, Asia and North America during the Ice Age.

Remains of these huge animals have been found in great numbers in places such as Siberia. Often their bodies have been found completely intact, as though they died recently. This is because the sub-zero temperatures prevented their flesh from deteriorating.

Does a skunk smell so bad?

Not only does a skunk smell bad, its spray can cause choking, and it can sting the eyes, causing temporary blindness. A skunk turns, raises its tail and squirts spray up to 3.5m (11ft 6in) from a gland beneath its tail.

Who was St Francis of Assisi?

He was born in the hillside town of Assisi, Italy in 1182. St Francis is the patron saint of animals, and he founded the order of Franciscans.

He led a wild life in his youth, then he changed - he took a vow of poverty, helped those in need and preached the Christian gospel.

What is an electric eel?

It's not an eel at all, but a freshwater fish, measuring up to 1.8m (6ft) long and related to the carp. The electric eel, which swims in the lakes and rivers of South America, can kill a human being as it releases a powerful 500 volt shock from electric organs in its body.

Is the Red Sea red?

The Red Sea owes its name to an algae that gives a red tinge to the water. This narrow inland sea is a branch of the Indian Ocean between north east Africa and the Arabian peninsula.

What is the Dead Sea?

It is a lake 369m (1,299ft) below sea level on the Israel/Jordan border. The water is seven times more salty than sea water. No fish can live in this water and swimmers float, but cannot sink.

How fast is a sneeze?

When something irritates the nerve endings of your nose you take a deep breath and sneeze at over 160km/h (100mph). Bless you!

Who invented jeans?

A sailmaker, Oscar Levi-Strauss, in San Francisco in 1850. The word 'jeans' may come from 'jene fustien', a strong twill cotton cloth, first made in Genoa. The original jeans were brown until blue denim was used.

Who was Madame Tussaud?

She was a French woman who made wax images from the death masks of royalty and aristocrats who had been beheaded by the guillotine during the French revolution.

The collection of wax works was founded in 1770 and brought to England in 1802. It has had a permanent home in London since 1835.

Was there a real Count Dracula?

Bram Stoker's novel about Dracula has been popular ever since 1897. Through films, plays, even comic books, everyone is familiar with Count Dracula, the bloodsucking vampire. The original Dracula may have been the 15th century prince Vlad Tepes. He was an evil, cruel man, but certainly not a vampire.

What is Transylvania?

In Romania, Transylvania is a wild rocky region in the Carpathian mountains. It covers an area of 55,166 sq. km (21,300 sq. miles).

What does the word 'Eskimo' mean?

The people of the Arctic are called Eskimo, which means 'eating it raw'.

Traditionally, they lived on a diet of raw fish, walrus, seal blubber and whale skin.

They prefer to call themselves 'Inuit', which means 'the people'.

Do peanuts grow on trees?

Peanuts (or ground nuts) are the seeds of a plant. The flower stalks bend over, bury themselves in the soil and the pods ripen underground.

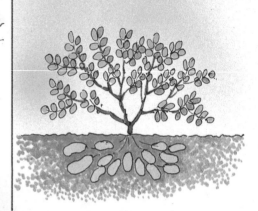

Can you bake Alaska?

This delicious dessert of ice cream on a cake base surrounded by meringue, then baked, was put together by New York chef, Charles Rahofer. This special sweet was to celebrate the American purchase of Alaska in 1867 from the Russians.

Which US president was a peanut farmer?

Jimmy Carter, the 39th President of the USA, was a naval officer and peanut farmer from Plains, Georgia.

What is the sound barrier?

As an aircraft flys it sends forward a pressure wave at the speed of sound.

If the plane flies at the same speed a shock wave of sound is produced called the 'sonic boom'.

What is an Oscar?

Oscar is the nickname of the golden statuette presented to people in the film industry for their work.

The Oscar ceremony is a glittering occasion with several Oscars being won annually.

The first of these trophies was presented in 1929. Four years later someone jokingly remarked that the statue looked like her Uncle Oscar - that name has been used ever since.

Was chewing gum invented in America?

Chewing gum was popular with the Mayans centuries ago. These central Americans chewed a gum-like latex from the chicle tree. Gum first came to the United States in 1860 and was flavoured with mint and aniseed.

What is the yeti?
Some people claim to have seen the yeti, a tall ape-like creature that is said to live high up in the Himalayas. Strange tracks found in the snow may belong to this animal, commonly known as the 'abominable snowman'.

Why does a candle burn?
When you light the wick of a candle the heat melts the wax and it creeps up the wick. As it meets the flame, wax vapour forms, mixes with oxygen in the air and burns!

Did you know that your body is two thirds water?
Every part of our body contains water. The weight of the adult human is made up of between 65 and 70% water, which is around 45 litres (79 pints).

Where were fireworks invented?
The Chinese had firework displays back in the 9th century. They used black gunpowder, a mixture of saltpetre, charcoal and sulphur. They fired rockets on very special occasions.

Which bird can smell with its beak?
The kiwi from New Zealand has nostrils at the tip of its beak. It sniffs out insects and worms and then pecks them out of the earth with its long beak.

Why is the sea salty?
Salt is a mineral that is gradually washed out of the rocks by rain and runs into the sea, making it taste salty. When sea water evaporates, salt is left behind.

What is the difference between a longbow and a crossbow?

The longbow is an ancient weapon. Originally made from one piece of wood, it could shoot an arrow over a long distance, making hunting much easier.

The crossbow is a small powerful bow, held and fired like a rifle. As a weapon of war it was deadly - it could pierce armour, but it was slow to reload.

Do you know what a totem pole is?

Among some Indians, certain creatures are believed to be the ancestors of the tribe. Totem animals are elaborately carved and painted on great wooden poles, often depicting the legends or exploits of the people.

What are pearls?

If a tiny grain of sand or grit gets inside an oyster, the creature protects itself by building a series of layers around the grain. The substance that forms these layers hardens to form a pearl.

What is amber?

It is fossilised resin from conifer trees that seeped out millions of years ago. Often insects were trapped inside. It lies buried until it is washed up on the seashore.

What is a pangolin?

A nocturnal scaly anteater. Most of its body is covered in yellow-brown scales. It rolls up like a ball and lives on ants and termites.

What is a geyser?

A hot spring that shoots a column of water and steam up into the air every so often. In volcanic regions water collects in deep cracks in the earth. It is heated by hot rocks and turns into steam that erupts with great force.

What is a shooting star?

It is really a meteor. Tiny rock particles flare up as they meet the atmosphere. They shoot across the sky, visible for a few seconds, then usually burn up.

Does a roadrunner really run?

Although the roadrunner can fly, it takes off at great speed to catch lizards and snakes, often running down the road. The roadrunner lives in the deserts of the USA and Mexico.

How did the leotard get its name?

This body-hugging garment worn by dancers and gymnasts was designed by Jules Leotard, a French trapeze artiste of the 1860s.

How does the flying fish fly?

This fish cannot fly like a bird, but it leaps into the air, up to 6m (20ft) then glides for about 400m (1,300ft) before splashing back.

Who built St Paul's Cathedral?

When he died in 1723 at the age of 90, Sir Christopher Wren had designed 50 churches in the city of London. His finest building was St Paul's Cathedral, which he built after the great fire of London.

The work began in 1675 and took 35 years to complete. The final stone was laid by Wren's son in 1710.

How much did St Paul's cost?

The total cost was £850,000. It was paid for by taxing all the boat loads of coal that arrived in the Port of London.

Where is the whispering gallery?

A gallery runs around the interior of the great dome of St Paul's. If you whisper inside this gallery your voice can be heard clearly on the opposite side, 34m (112ft) away.

Where is the Wren Memorial?

Above Wren's tomb in St. Paul's are written these words, "Reader, if you seek his monument, look about you!"

When was the great fire?

It began early in the morning of Sunday September 2nd 1666, at the house of a baker in Pudding Lane. The fire burned for three days, devastating the city of London. Many houses were built of wood, so the fire spread rapidly. In the end gunpowder was used to blow up some streets, producing gaps too wide for the flames to leap across. By this time, 460 streets had been destroyed, nearly 90 churches and 13,000 houses.

What is the Tower of London?

A fortress on the bank of the Thames. The oldest part is the keep or the White Tower, built in 1078 by William the Conqueror on the site of an earlier Roman fortress. For centuries it was used as a royal residence and a state prison.

Which treasure is kept in the Tower?

The Crown jewels or regalia, used by the King or Queen on state occasions, are kept in vaults under the Waterloo Barracks. They include eight crowns, sceptres, orbs and the coronation ring. The imperial state crown has nearly 3,000 diamonds.

Some of the Crown jewels of Great Britain

Why are ravens kept there?

According to legend, Britain will be invaded if the ravens leave the Tower. Charles II passed a royal charter ordering at least six ravens to be kept there at all times.

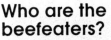

Who are the beefeaters?

The yeoman warders or beefeaters (French word, 'boufitiers', guardians of the king's buffet) were formed in 1485 by Henry VII. There are about 40 of them living and working in the Tower.

39

How old are the first human footprints?

They were made 3.75 million years ago by a group of early human-like creatures as they walked across a strip of volcanic ash near the Olduvai Gorge in Tanzania, Africa. The ash dried and became hard, which preserved the footprints until they were found in 1976.

Do turtles have teeth?

Turtles and tortoises do not have teeth. Their jaws have razor-sharp edges to cut up and shred their food.

What is a loofah?

The bathroom loofah is the dried centre of a vegetable called the luffa.

It is a member of the gourd family of plants and related to the pumpkin and the cucumber.

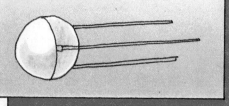

Who is Nanook?

The Eskimos call the polar bear 'Nanook', which means 'ice-bear'. These huge bears that roam the Arctic often weigh up to 600kg (1,323lb) and stand around 3.5m (11.5ft) tall.

Who launched the first satellite?

On October 4th 1957, Russia launched the first man-made satellite into space. It was known as Sputnik-1. The satellite was a sphere 56cm (22in) in diameter and weighed 83.6kg (185lb).

Who played golf on the Moon?

US astronaut Alan Shepherd, the commander of Apollo 14, played the first golf shot on the Moon in 1971.

Who went for the first drive on the Moon?

On July 31st 1971, astronauts David Scott and James Irwin (two of the crew of Apollo 15) drove for several miles across the bumpy surface of the Moon. They rode in their lunar roving vehicle or 'moon buggy'

How much honey comes from a hive?

An average colony of bees in a hive (about 60,000 worker bees) can produce around 25kg (1lb) of pure honey in a year.

Do all bees sting?

Only female bees can sting. A bee's sting is like a sharp thorn at the end of its abdomen. If the thorn is left in your flesh, the bee cannot sting again!

What happened to King Midas?

In Greek mythology, Midas was granted a wish by the god Dionysus. Midas asked that everything he touched should turn to gold.

At first it was wonderful, but when he reached for food and drink, and that turned to gold, he soon began to starve. When he touched his beloved daughter and she turned to gold too, he begged for his wish to be taken back!

What is Reuters?

It is an organisation whose agents supply newspapers with news from all over the world. It was founded in Germany in 1849 by a man named Reuter. At first he sent his messages by pigeon post until the telegraph was invented.

What is an ermine?

In cold climates the red-brown fur of the stoat turns white in winter. It is then known as an ermine. The white fur with its distinctive black-tipped tail is used on some ceremonial robes.

Which animal can sleep on its back?

Humans are the only animals that can do this!

How is a watermark made?

When paper is made, wet pulp is spread on fine wire gauze to dry. Some of the wires can be arranged to form words or designs that appear on the paper as a watermark. Hold the paper up to the light and see!

What does G.M.T. stand for?

G.M.T. is short for Greenwich Mean Time. It is the scientific standard of time for the whole world. The BBC broadcast the Greenwich time signal on the radio. Every hour, on the hour, you can count the six bleeps or 'pips'. The last pip sounds exactly on the hour!

Who was Neptune?

He was the Roman god of the sea. To the Greeks he was known as Poseidon. With his three-pronged trident he is said to control the wind and the waves.

Who rode in the first hot-air balloon?

Before the French Montgolfier brothers made their first manned flight in a hot-air balloon in 1783, they sent a duck, a cock and a sheep up first. They wanted to find out if the animals would be harmed by the thinner air.

What shook San Francisco?

In April 1906, a great earthquake and fire destroyed over a third of the city. Over 100,000 people were made homeless in the 30-second tremor. San Francisco is built on the San Andreas Fault, so this could happen any time!

Do birds have teeth?

No they don't. The structure of birds' bodies must be light. Strong jaw bones and teeth would add weight to a bird's skull and this would make flying difficult.

When did the first birds live on Earth?

About 150 million years ago there lived a bird-like creature called an archaeopteryx. It had feathers, wings and a head like a lizard with sharp teeth instead of a beak. It was about as big as a seagull.

What is the best way to keep warm?

Wear several layers of clothing. Air is trapped between the layers, and this helps you to keep warm.

Who founded the Boy Scouts?

The Scout movement was formed by Lord Baden-Powell, whose book *Scouting for Boys* appeared in 1908. This movement has spread throughout the world.

Lord Baden-Powell and his sister founded the Girl Guide organisation in 1910.

Is a mole blind?

A mole has very poor eyesight, but is not blind. Its tiny eyes are hidden deep in its fur.

The mole burrows under the surface of the ground in search of worms and insects. It has a huge appetite and cannot live for more than 12 hours without food.

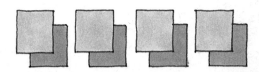

How did we get the word 'alphabet'?

From the first two letters of the Greek alphabet, 'alpha' and 'beta'.

What creature hides behind a trap-door?

The trap-door spider digs a tunnel and covers it with a trap-door. It hides underneath with the trap-door slightly open. When its prey comes along it jumps out and grabs it!

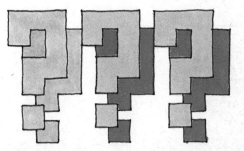

What is the Colosseum?

A great amphitheatre in Rome completed in AD80. It was a huge stadium for chariot races, gladiator fighting and even mock sea battles. The Romans enjoyed games in which people and wild animals were killed in the most cruel ways. Admission was free even to slaves. There were seats for more than 80,000 people and standing room for 20,000 more.

The Colosseum is now in ruins and is one of the sights of Rome.

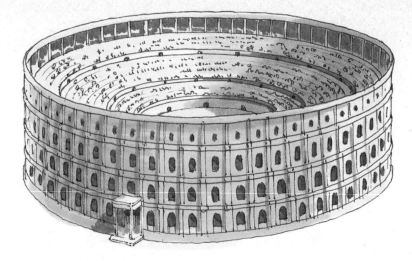

Who were the gladiators?

They were men who fought in the arena to entertain the ancient Romans. Usually they were slaves, prisoners of war or criminals - a few were volunteers.

There were different kinds of gladiators. Some wore armour with helmets and shields, and fought with a sword or an axe; some were armed with a trident and a net; others used a noose.

Most contests were fought to the death, but gladiators who survived many battles became heroes and retired as wealthy men.

When the defeated gladiator was not killed during a fight, it was the custom for the crowd to signal with their thumbs whether his life should be spared. Thumbs up meant that he should live; thumbs down meant that he should die.

42

Who were the samurai?

The samurai were the old warrior class of Japan. From an early age children were taught to fight using a curved two-handed sword called a katana. Each warrior also carried a smaller sword called a wakizashi. Their other main weapon was the longbow.

These fierce warriors were also trained in artistic skills such as poetry, writing and flower arranging!

What was their armour made of?

Suits of armour with great helmets were mainly ceremonial. The fighting man wore lightweight armour made of small metal plates fastened together with coloured cards.

What was a shogun?

The shogun was the military ruler of old Japan. Japan was always ruled by emperors who claimed to be descended from the gods. But as the samurai lords became more powerful, the emperors became more of a religious figurehead. The real power in the land was held by the strongest of the samurai leaders who took the title of shogun.

Do the samurai still exist?

Japan remained an almost closed country living in the past, until 1854 when a treaty was signed with the United States. After that the samurai had no real place in Japan and ended in 1877.

Which famous skyscraper did King Kong climb?

It was the Empire State Building in New York, a skyscraper office block completed in 1931. For 40 years this 102 storey, 381m (1,250ft) high building was the tallest in the world. From the top you can see for 130km (80miles).

In the film *King Kong* (1933) the citizens of New York were terrorised by a huge ape that climbed to the top of the skyscraper and was finally shot down by US army fighter planes.

Who was the first man in space?

The Russian major Yuri Alexeyevitch Gagarin became the first man to fly in space on April 12th 1961. His spaceship Vostock orbited the Earth for 108 minutes before returning.

He was killed at the age of 34 in 1968 when the MIG-15 jet trainer he was flying crashed.

What is mistletoe?

This evergreen plant is a parasite, growing on the branches of various forest and fruit trees. Mistletoe was sacred to the people of ancient Europe. Druids used it in their sacrifices and the Celts believed it had magical and healing powers.

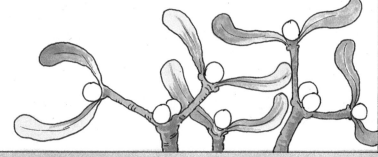

What is the Bayeaux Tapestry?

It is an embroidery, commissioned for Bayeaux Cathedral in Calvados, France. It shows the conquest of England by the Norman King, William I in 1066.

It is worked in eight colours on a band of linen 70.4m (231ft) long, and 50cm (20in) deep.

The story of the Norman invasion is told in 72 scenes, starting with the English King Harold's visit to the Norman Court and ending with his death at Hastings, shot through the eye by an arrow.

The tapestry can still be seen at Bayeaux.

What is the world's highest mountain?

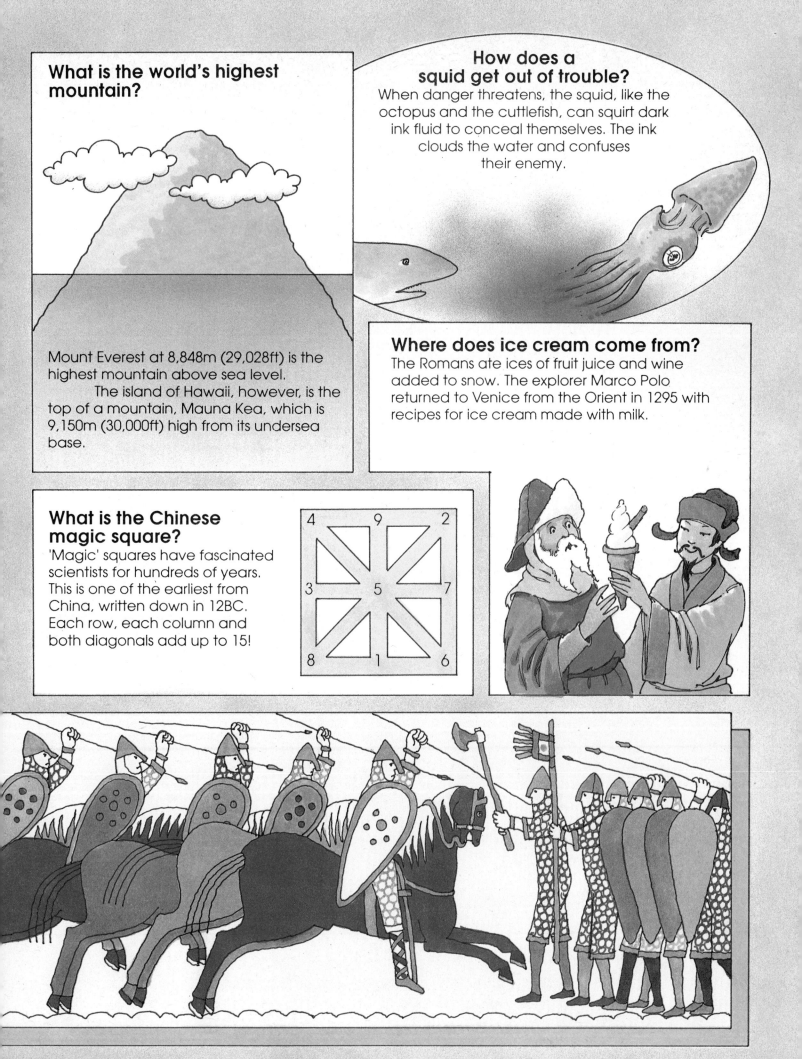

Mount Everest at 8,848m (29,028ft) is the highest mountain above sea level.

The island of Hawaii, however, is the top of a mountain, Mauna Kea, which is 9,150m (30,000ft) high from its undersea base.

How does a squid get out of trouble?

When danger threatens, the squid, like the octopus and the cuttlefish, can squirt dark ink fluid to conceal themselves. The ink clouds the water and confuses their enemy.

Where does ice cream come from?

The Romans ate ices of fruit juice and wine added to snow. The explorer Marco Polo returned to Venice from the Orient in 1295 with recipes for ice cream made with milk.

What is the Chinese magic square?

'Magic' squares have fascinated scientists for hundreds of years. This is one of the earliest from China, written down in 12BC. Each row, each column and both diagonals add up to 15!

4	9	2
3	5	7
8	1	6

What is a vacuum?

A space that contains absolutely nothing! Scientists believe that it is impossible to have a complete vacuum - an empty space with no air or substance whatsoever.

So a vacuum as we know it, is an enclosed space from which as much air and matter as possible has been removed.

A thermos flask has a double wall inside, with a vacuum between the two walls. Hot liquid is kept hot because the heat cannot pass through the vacuum by convection or conduction.

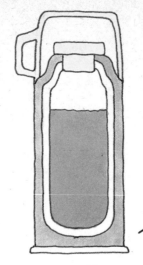

What is shorthand?

Shorthand is a quick way of writing. Words are represented by simple strokes and symbols.

Early shorthand was first used in 63BC. Modern shorthand was invented by Pitman in 1837 and a system devised by Gregg has been in use in America since 1888.

Which bird catches fish for people to eat?

A web-footed diving bird, the cormorant, with a huge appetite for fish. In the East, fishermen use the cormorant to dive underwater to catch fish for them. A metal ring around the bird's neck stops it from swallowing the fish.

How can cats see in the dark?

No animal can see in total darkness, but when the light is poor, cats can enlarge (dilate) the pupils of their eyes. This means that more light is admitted to the eye.

Owls use this technique as well.

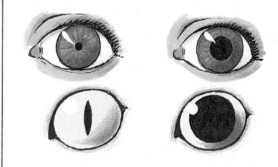

How much of the world's natural water is in the oceans?

Water is nature's most plentiful liquid.

Three quarters of the Earth is covered in it, and 97% of all the world's water flows in the oceans. The polar ice caps hold another 2% and the remainder goes round and round in the world's water cycle forever, evaporating and falling again as rain or snow.

Why do animals' eyes shine in the dark?

Many animals have a layer of crystalline substance in their eyes that reflects light. When their eyes shine it is just the reflection of other lights, a car's headlights or perhaps the street lights.

Which US president was born in a log cabin?

Abraham Lincoln, the 16th president of the USA was born on February 16th 1809 in a log cabin on the Kentucky frontier. Lincoln grew up on a farm in Indiana. He educated himself and became a lawyer, and in 1861 he was elected president.

What is an illuminated manuscript?

Before the invention of printing, all books were copied by hand. Monks and scribes laboriously wrote out the text in pen on parchment. Often single letters, words and borders were decorated or illuminated in these manuscripts.

When was dormouse on the menu?

The Romans really did eat dormice! They were stuffed with minced pork, pepper, pine kernels and garlic, placed on a tile and baked in the oven. The recipe dates back to the first century BC.

Which country does this flag belong to?

It is not one country's flag, but the flag of the European Community. No one could decide on a new flag for Europe, so in 1986 the EC adopted the Council of Europe's flag.

Who ate their plates at dinner time?

In the Middle Ages you could eat your plate if you were really hungry, because it was a thick slice of unleavened bread. Usually it was given to the poor or the dogs at the end of a meal.

Which great musician was deaf?

Ludwig Van Beethoven, born in Bonn in 1790, was one of the world's greatest composers. He began to lose his hearing at the age of 26, and by 1823 he was completely deaf. Beethoven never heard his nine symphonies or piano concertos, or any of his other compositions during the last ten years of his life.

Where is Poet's Corner?

It is in the south transept of Westminster Abbey. In 1956 a monument was erected there to Geoffrey Chaucer (1340-1400), one of the first poets to write in the English language. His poems *The Canterbury Tales* are about a band of pilgrims who travel from London to the shrine of Thomas à Becket at Canterbury. During their pilgrimage each traveller tells a story. Since Chaucer it has been a great honour for a poet to be commemorated in Poet's Corner.

Who is buried there?

Few poets are actually buried in the abbey, but Chaucer, Shakespeare, Milton, Wordsworth, Keats, Shelley and Ben Jonson are remembered in Poet's Corner.

Who was Icarus?

In Greek mythology, Icarus and his father Daedalus tried to escape from the island of Crete by flying away on wings made of feathers and wax. Icarus flew too close to the Sun, the wax melted and he plunged into the Aegean sea and drowned.

Why do we blush?

When our cheeks go red with embarrassment, shame, or even pleasure, people say we are blushing!

Tiny blood vessels (capillaries) under the skin open wide to let lots of blood run through. Blushing is one of the ways the body has for keeping the blood it sends to the brain at the correct temperature.

Why do we turn pale when frightened?

Your face turns white because blood is diverted to another part of your body. The heart pumps faster and stronger pushing blood to the limb muscles and adrenaline is released into the bloodstream. In fact, your body is getting itself ready to run or even fight.

When danger is past the body quickly returns to normal.

Who was Ned Kelly?

He was a famous Australian bandit or bushranger, the leader of the outlawed Kelly gang. Although he was a bank robber and defied the police for years, Ned Kelly was admired and thought of as a hero!

He wore strange iron armour made from a plough share. In 1880 he was finally captured and his gang were killed. Later Kelly was hanged and became a legend.

Is a sea anemone a plant?

No, it is an animal that attaches itself to rocks. The anemone seizes and paralyses shrimps and shellfish with its waving tentacles before pulling them into its mouth to be digested.

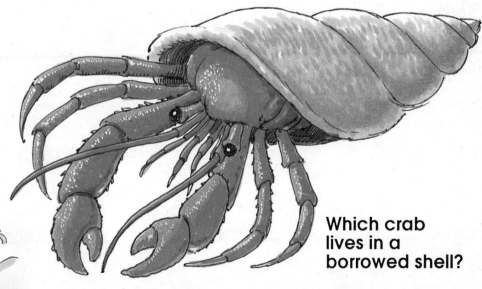

Which crab lives in a borrowed shell?

Hermit crabs use abandoned mollusc shells as homes. This crab's abdomen is soft, so the extra shell is for protection. When the crab grows it simply finds a bigger shell to live in.

Who built the Taj Mahal?

The Mogul emperor Shah Jahan had one of the most beautiful buildings in the world built at Agra in India, as a tomb for his beloved wife Mumtaz Mahal. She had 14 children and died when she was 39.

From 1630, over a period of 20 years, 20,000 men worked on the white marble tomb. The walls were inlaid with 12 different kinds of semi-precious stones and carved inscriptions from the Koran.

Today people can visit the Taj Mahal between the hours of dawn and dusk. It is just outside the city of Delhi in northern India.

What happened to Shah Jahan?

Shah Jahan was born in 1592 and died in 1666. He became emperor in 1628 and during his reign some of the finest monuments of Mogul architecture were built.

When Shah Jahan had finished building his wife's tomb, he planned to build an identical one in black marble for himself. It was to stand on the opposite bank of the River Jumna from the Taj Mahal, connected by a silver bridge.

Sadly, his own son imprisoned him in this palace before it was complete and the Indian emperor died there. Now his tomb lies in the Taj Mahal beside his wife Mumtaz.

Which American presidents are carved into a mountain?

In the Black Hills of Dakota, USA, is the site of Mount Rushmore National Memorial, covering 13 sq. km (5 sq. miles). These giant heads took Gutzon Borglum 15 years to carve out of the face of the mountain. They represent four American presidents: Washington, Jefferson, Lincoln and Theodore Roosevelt. The heads from chin to top are 18m (60ft) high.

Which building looks like a sailing ship?

The white curved roof of the Sydney Opera House was designed to look like the billowing sails of a ship sailing in the waters of Sydney Harbour.

Danish architect Jorn Utzon won an international contest with his design for the Opera House and work began in 1957. It was completed 16 years later, having cost 14 times more than the original estimate. Most of the extra cash was raised by a series of Opera House lotteries.

If you visit the Opera House you must park and then take a bus for 1.6km (1 mile), as there is no car park!

Who were the Aztecs?

They were a race of Indians who were living in the plains of central and southern America.

The Aztecs were a wandering people until 1324 when they settled in a marshy village called Tenochtitlan. Legend says that it is the place where they found an eagle on a cactus eating a serpent, and that is where their gods told them to build a great city. Tenochtitlan grew into just that. As well as a magnificent city, the Aztecs built a great pyramid-shaped temple where they carried out hundreds of human sacrifices, cutting out the hearts as an offering to their gods.

But in 1519 the Spaniard, Cortés led an expedition into Mexico. In less than two years he had killed the Aztec leader Montezuma and destroyed their city. Cortés had better weapons, and soldiers mounted on horseback - the Aztecs were terrified, as they had never seen a horse before. Soon they were defeated and Mexico was claimed for Spain.

Today the Aztec city of Tenochtitlan lies beneath modern Mexico City. The Great Temple has been excavated and the site can be visited today.

The Aztec God Quetzalcoatl

Who were the Incas?

This was the name of the people who lived in the mountains of Peru before the arrival of the Spaniards.

The Incas called themselves 'children of the Sun', which they worshipped as a god. They mined gold and silver and made it into beautiful statues, masks and ornaments. They built roads around the steep mountain sides, connecting them by rope and vine bridges. No vehicles ever used these routes, as the Incas did not have the wheel!

This great civilisation came to a swift end when the Spaniards came in search of land and gold. The Spanish conquistador, Pizarro, marched into Peru with 180 men and 37 horses to conquer the country. He captured the Inca ruler Atahualpa, and accepted a room full of gold for the ruler to be returned to his people. But after the Spaniards had taken the gold, they put Atahualpa to death.

Within a few years, the whole of the Inca empire and all its treasures belonged to Spain. Very few of the golden statues and ornaments can be seen today as the Spaniards melted them down into ingots.

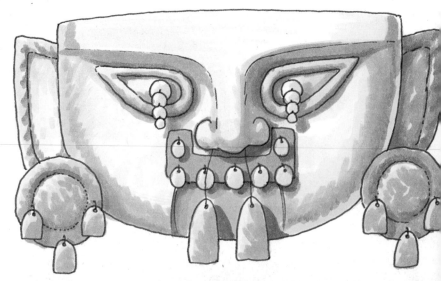

Inca funeral mask of gold

Can you see an Inca city today?

Machu Picchu is a ruined city that the Incas abandoned. It stands on a mountain ridge high in the south western Andes. This ancient city was undiscovered until 1911, when an American archaeologist, Hiram Bingham, was the first to see it.

If you ever travel to Peru, you can walk around the ruined houses and terraces of Machu Picchu.

Who were Romulus and Remus?

They are part of a famous legend about the founding of Rome.

As babies, the twin boys Romulus and Remus were left in their cradle to drown in the River Tiber. They were rescued by a she-wolf and later found by a shepherd. When they grew up they decided to found a city, but quarrelled over the choice of site, and Remus was killed. When the city was built, Romulus named it Rome - after himself.

Who was Hercules?

He was a famous hero of Greek mythology. Hercules was well known for his great strength and courage. While still in his cradle, he strangled two serpents that were sent to kill him.

As the legend goes, when he became a man he was set 12 impossible tasks, known as the 12 labours. One of the tasks was to clean out the Augean stables, in which King Augeas had kept 3,000 cattle for 30 years. Hercules cleaned the stables in one day by diverting two rivers through them.

When all 12 of his tasks were finished, he set sail with Jason and the Argonauts to find the Golden Fleece.

After his death, because of his many brave adventures, Hercules became a god.

What was a minotaur?

In Greek mythology it was a monstrous creature that was half-man, half-bull. The minotaur was kept in the middle of a labyrinth or maze, by King Minos of Crete. Every year it killed seven young men and sent seven young women from Athens as a sacrifice.

One year a boy named Theseus volunteered to join the young men and try to kill the minotaur.

With the help of Ariadne (daughter of King Minos) he found his way into the maze, and bravely killed the monster.

He was able to find his way out of the labyrinth as Ariadne had given him a ball of thread to mark his path.

How talented was the young Mozart?

Little Wolfgang Amadeus Mozart could play the harpsichord at the age of three. He composed music at the age of five, and some of those tunes he wrote still survive today.

In 1762, when he was only six, he played in concerts in Munich and Vienna with his 11-year-old sister Maria Anna.

For the next few years the two children travelled all over Europe giving concerts, often in front of royalty.

When he was 21, the Austrian Emperor asked Mozart to write his first opera, and the Archbishop of Salzburg made the young boy leader of his court orchestra. By the time he was 15, he had already composed 13 symphonies. During his short lifetime he wrote over 600 works, but Mozart earned very little money from his music and was often in debt.

He died in 1791 at the age of 35. Mozart, who was probably the greatest musician that ever lived, was buried in an unmarked grave in St Mark's cemetery, Vienna.

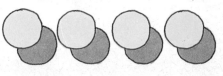

Can a bird fly all of the time?

Most birds fly for short periods and then return to land to rest and feed. There are some birds that can fly non-stop for years. The sooty tern flies over the oceans for 3-10 years before returning to land to breed.

Which bird builds an oven?

The oven bird gets its name from the strong, oven-shaped nest that it builds up from layers of mud.

Can birds fly backwards?

Humming birds can! These tiny birds with their high speed wing beats can fly in any direction, even backwards. They can also keep their bodies perfectly still in mid-air.

Which bird flies underwater?

On land the flightless penguin is a clumsy, funny creature. Underwater it 'flies' with great speed and grace.

Which bird has the largest wingspan?

The wandering albatross spends its life flying over the southern oceans. With its 3.5m (12ft) wingspan, it glides over the waves stopping only to feed.

Which bird goes to prison?

The female hornbill is sealed into her nest in a hollow made by the male. He does this to protect both her and the eggs from dangers such as monkeys.

What is bird's-nest soup?

This Chinese delicacy is made by soaking and cooking the nests of a type of swift. The bird makes its nest with saliva.

Which bird can weave?

The male red-headed weaverbird makes a large nest by weaving grasses together. These strong nests may last for a year and can be used many times.

Did you know that a bird can sew?

The tailorbird makes a nest using its sharp beak as a needle to sew two large leaves together. The leaves are then filled with soft grasses.

Did you know that the peregrine falcon can dive at over 320km/h (200mph)?

This is the fastest bird in flight, but it would not be able to dive on its prey at this speed.

55

Who was Genghis Khan?

The Mongol ruler who built up the vast Mongol empire in the early 1200s.

Genghis Khan and his armies terrorised people with their violence and cruelty, but to his people he was God's representative on Earth, their supreme ruler.

He formed armies of horsemen, and after many victories whole armies came to join him. His fierce Mongol soldiers conquered most of northern China by breaking through the Great Wall. His empire stretched right across Asia and into Eastern Europe and Russia.

Who invented dynamite and left his money to peace?

Alfred Nobel, a Swedish chemist, invented dynamite in 1867 and gelignite in 1875.

During his early experiments his laboratory blew up, killing Nobel's younger brother and four workers.

Nobel made a huge fortune out of the manufacture of explosives and left the biggest part of the money for annual awards called Nobel Prizes. The seven prizes are for physics, chemistry, economics, physiology or medicine, literature and peace.

Who was Harry Houdini?

His real name was Erik Weiss and he was the most famous escapologist of all time. He could escape from locked handcuffs, straitjackets, even sealed, underwater boxes.

What was the deepest ocean dive?

This took place in 1960 when three members of the US navy descended into the 10,916m (35,800ft) deep Marianas Trench in the Pacific. They made the dive in a bathyscaphe called 'Trieste'.

What is the difference between a tortoise and a terrapin?

The shell of a tortoise is heavier and more dome-shaped than the terrapin's. Neither reptiles have teeth, but their jaws are razor sharp.

A terrapin has a more streamlined shape than a tortoise. It can live in fresh water as well as on land. Some of them have slightly webbed feet.

How do parrots stay on their perches while they sleep?

A bird has tendons in its feet that go up into the leg. When it perches the tendons are pulled tight and this makes the bird's toes curl around the perch in a tight grasp.

Who was the first person to reach the South Pole?

In December 1911, the Norwegian explorer Roald Amundsen won the race to the South Pole with four men and their dog teams. They reached the pole 34 days ahead of Captain Scott, whose party all died on the way home.

Is there really a Loch Ness monster?

Underwater cameras, frogmen and even submarines have searched the 37km (23 miles) of Loch Ness in vain. In 1960 a few seconds of film recorded something travelling across the surface of the water. Could Nessie really be a survivor from prehistory?

Who invented cornflakes?

Will Keith Kellogg discovered cornflakes by accident in 1894. His brother was a doctor looking for a food that was easy for patients to digest. Will boiled a pan of wheat and from its contents thought up the idea of cornflakes.

What happened to the Titanic?

On April 5th 1912 the Titanic was on her maiden voyage to New York when disaster struck! This great ship, said to be unsinkable, struck an iceberg and sank within two and half hours. More than 1,500 passengers and crew were drowned in the north Atlantic's freezing waters. Only 712 survived.

    The Titanic was hoping to win the Blue Riband for the fastest Atlantic crossing!

Which animal is a worldwide symbol?

The World Wildlife Fund (WWF) for nature campaigns to protect wildlife and habitats all over the world. Its symbol is the giant panda.

Where do pandas live?

In isolated parts of China, high up in the mountains. They are very rare, and live alone in areas of bamboo forest.

Why do some creatures become extinct?

When a species dies out it disappears forever. Humans are often responsible for hunting and killing some animals to extinction, like the passenger pigeon, the last of which died in a zoo.

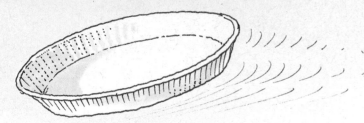

Who invented the frisbee?

In 1871 an American pie maker called Mr Frisbee supplied Yale University with pies in tins. The students ate the pies and threw the cases at each other. In 1948 the first plastic frisbee appeared.

Why do falcons wear hoods?

In falconry the birds are trained to catch prey and bring it back to the handler.

The falcon is hooded so that it is not distracted as it perches on the gloved wrist of the falconer. When the hood is removed the bird takes off in search of game.

Does coffee grow on trees?

It grows on an evergreen shrub in hot climates. Two seeds or beans grow inside a red cherry-like fruit. These beans are roasted and then ground to make coffee.

What is an avalanche?

When a mass of snow builds up on a mountain and then begins to slip it falls rapidly down the mountainside.

Often the slightest sound or movement can send thousands of tonnes of snow crashing down. A large avalanche can bury everything in its path.

Did Robin Hood really live in Sherwood Forest?

This legendary hero was said to have lived in Sherwood Forest, Nottinghamshire during the reign of Richard I who was King from 1189-1199.

During this time, Richard the Lionheart was away from England on crusades in the holy land and neglected his duties as King. He left his brother Prince John in charge of the country who, together with the Sheriff of Nottingham, declared Robin Hood an outlaw.

According to legend, Robin then became the leader of an outlaw band dressed in Lincoln green and armed with longbows, who robbed the rich to help the poor.

From the 14th century onwards, tales and ballads of this popular hero began to appear, but no one has really been able to prove that Robin Hood existed.

Was St George English?

Since medieval times, St George's Day has been celebrated on April 23rd. Although St George is the patron saint of England, he is thought to have come from North America. He may have been a Roman soldier, put to death for his Christian faith around AD300.

Legend says that St George came riding into a land where the people were terrorised by a dragon. Its next victim was to be the King's daughter. As the dragon was about to devour her, St George attacked and killed it with an iron lance.

Tales of this mysterious knight spread, and he became the saint of the medieval crusaders as well as the patron saint of many places - Venice, Portugal, parts of Spain and England. His special flag is a red cross on a white background.

Did King Arthur ever rule Britain?

As a boy of 15, Arthur pulled out a sword embedded in a great anvil, when everyone else had failed. This test proved that he was the rightful King of England.

At his court in Camelot, Arthur ruled with his Queen Guinevere, advised by Merlin the magician. His knights were devoted to a life of chivalry and sat equally placed at the Round Table.

Throughout his life Arthur carried a magic sword, Excalibur, given to him by the Lady of the Lake. On his death the sword was thrown back into the lake, out of which an arm appeared, took the sword and vanished!

The legend may have been based on a British warrior who fought the Saxons after the Romans left. Camelot could be Winchester, and Cornwall is thought to be the home of the legends of King Arthur.

Why did the Pied Piper take the children of Hamelin?

In 1284 the town of Hamelin in Germany was plagued by rats.

One day an odd looking piper appeared offering to rid the town of rats, and the Mayor gladly agreed to pay him. As he played his pipe, the rats followed the stranger towards the river, where they fell in and drowned.

When the Piper asked for his fee, the Mayor refused. As the piper played once more, all the children of the town followed him, dancing towards Koppelberg mountain. An enormous cavern opened up, the children ran inside and were never seen again!

Who shot an apple on his son's head?

In Switzerland in the 13th century, the Austrian governor Gessler ordered everyone to salute a hat placed by him on a pole in the market square. William Tell refused and was ordered to split an apple placed on his son's head with one arrow - or be killed!

Tell succeeded, but said he had a second arrow ready to kill Gessler if he had missed the apple and killed his son. As a result he was imprisoned, but he later escaped, shot Gessler and became a hero.

What is the forbidden city?

The forbidden city is in Beijing (Peking). In 1421, the third emperor of the Ming dynasty laid out his imperial walled capital like a series of boxes one inside the other.

First came the outer city, then the inner city, next the imperial city and last of all the forbidden city. Ordinary people entered on pain of death. Nowadays it is open to ordinary tourists.

What is a centipede?

Centipedes' bodies are made up of many segments, each with one pair of legs. Although the word 'centipede' means 100 feet, some of these meat-eating creatures can have as little as 15 pairs of legs, or as many as 177 pairs.

And what is a millipede?

The millipede, like the centipede, is not an insect, nor does it have a thousand feet. It has a worm-like segmented body with up to 240 legs.

Young millipedes have only six legs but extra legs grow as they mature.

Why do we shiver?

When you are very cold you shiver uncontrollably! Your muscles shake all over because this is the body's way of warming you up.

What was the world's first postage stamp?

The Penny Black was first used in England in May 1840. Six million were printed in unperforated sheets of 240. Post Office staff had to cut the stamps into strips. It cost one penny to deliver a letter, whatever the distance.

Who celebrates Thanksgiving Day?

This day falls on the last Thursday in November. It is an annual national holiday in the USA, a traditional thanksgiving for the year's harvest.

The first Thanksgiving was celebrated by the Pilgrim Fathers in 1621 and lasted three whole days. The settlers and their Indian friends ate wild turkey, geese, duck, lobsters, clams, oysters and popcorn.

Where do turkeys come from?

These large wild game birds come from the USA. Early European settlers almost wiped out the turkey in North America because it became one of their favourite foods.

Who was the messenger of the gods?

Mercury was the mythological messenger of the Roman gods, his Greek name was Hermes. He wore a winged hat and winged sandals and carried a herald's wand intertwined with snakes or ribbon.

What is a secretary bird?

This African bird gets its name from the long feathers on its head, which resemble old fashioned quill pens. It runs swiftly after snakes, and kills them with its powerful legs.

Who first made paper?

Paper was first made by wasps! They make paper for their nests by chewing up fragments of wood.

The ancient Egyptians made paper from a water reed called papyrus - hence the name paper.

As early as the second century the Chinese manufactured paper from bamboo fibres, pounded and pulped and then left to dry.

Who invented frozen food?

Throughout history people living in sub-zero temperatures have always preserved their food by leaving it outside until it was frozen solid.

It wasn't until 1924 that food was frozen commercially. An American scientist named Clarence Birdseye went on an expedition to Labrador. He noticed fish and venison being eaten by the Eskimos. When thawed, cooked and eaten, the food lost none of its taste.

Back in America, Birdseye discovered a mechanical method of quick-freezing food. But it was very slow and he could freeze no more than 500 tonnes of fruit and vegetables a year.

Over the next few years he improved his freezing machinery, and on June 6th 1930, a group of Massachusetts' grocers offered boxes of frozen peas for sale!

When was Coca-Cola first tasted?

This world famous drink was invented over a hundred years ago by John Pemberton, a chemist from Atlanta, Georgia.

In 1886 he made up a syrup of cola-nut extract, caffeine, cocoa leaves, vegetable extracts and sugar.

One day his assistant diluted some of this syrup with soda-water, then served it to a customer in Pemberton's drugstore. This was the first Coca-Cola ever tasted.

The famous Coca-Cola trademark was originally the beautiful handwriting of Pemberton's business partner Frank Robertson.

How did the St Bernard dog get its name?

These huge, strong dogs were originally from the Swiss Alps. They were trained to dig out travellers lost or buried in snowdrifts as they crossed mountain passes.

It is a popular belief that the small barrel of brandy round the St Bernard's neck, was to revive any freezing survivors that the dogs might rescue. However, it was Sir Edwin Landseer (Queen Victoria's favourite artist) who added the barrel to one of his paintings, and people have believed the story ever since!

What is the Victoria Cross?

The highest British decoration for bravery by members of the armed services during a war. It was first instituted by Queen Victoria at the end of the Crimean War.

The medal is a Maltese Cross in bronze and for many years was made from cannon captured at Sevastopol.

What is the Purple Heart?

Since 1932, American servicemen wounded in battle have often received the Purple Heart, but it was back in 1782 that George Washington first introduced this award. Then, soldiers who displayed 'gallantry and faith' could stitch a purple heart-shaped patch of cloth onto their uniform.

For a hundred and fifty years this award was forgotten. Then it was revived in the 1930s!

How old is Mr Punch?

Mr Punch is thought to originate from an old Italian puppet called Pulcinella, first created around 1600 by Silvio Fiorillo, a comedian.

In 1662 Samuel Pepys saw Punchinello (later shortened to Punch) in London's Covent Garden for the first time. He wrote in his famous diary on May 9th that the puppet show was wonderful.

Punch and Judy shows were very popular in Victorian times. Charles Dickens mentions them in four of his novels.

In France Mr Punch is known as Polichinelle, and in Russia he is called Petrushka.

How did the piano get its name?

In 1710 the Italian, Bartolomeo Cristofori created the first pianoforte. Its name comes from two Italian words, 'piano' ('soft') and 'forte' ('loud').

Earlier instruments like the harpsichord had quills that plucked the strings when the keys were played, but the volume of the notes was the same.

On the new pianoforte, strings of different lengths were struck with felt-covered hammers. Hit the note hard and the hammer would make a louder note, touch the note gently and the music would play softly!

A piano can make notes of different volume according to the force with which the keys are struck.

Who were the first people to keep cats?

The ancient Egyptians kept cats more than 4,000 years ago. Their goddess Bastet was shown as a cat or cat-headed woman. To them, the cat was a sacred animal. Killing a cat, even by accident, was punishable by death!

If a pet cat died, the whole family would shave off their eyebrows as a sign of mourning. The Egyptians mummified their cats and buried them in special vaults, often with mummified mice!

Does milk come from cows?

Milk is one of our most complete foods, and one of the most important foods worldwide, but not all of it comes from cows!

Goats' milk is more easily digested than cows' milk. Water-buffalo milk is very rich. Ewes' milk is used in France to make Roquefort cheese. In Tibet they drink yaks' milk, and in Lapland reindeers' milk. Arabs milk their camels and Mongolians drink mares' milk.

Does milk come from trees?

Coconuts have a double shell and inside the inner rough brown shell of a fresh coconut you will find a sweet milk. If you pierce the 'eyes' of the nut with a skewer, you can drain the liquid into a bowl ready to drink!

Who first played the game of baseball?

The American game of baseball almost certainly came from England many years ago.

It was mentioned in 1700, when a vicar in Kent wrote how much he hated the game being played on a Sunday!

In one of Jane Austen's novels of 1798, she wrote that one of her characters preferred cricket, baseball and horse-riding to reading books!

In England, hundreds of years before this, children enjoyed playing rounders - a game very similar to baseball. When the first English colonists came to settle in America in the 1660s, they may have brought rounders with them - which eventually became baseball!

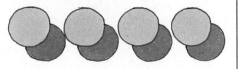

Can crabs climb trees?

The robber crab can easily climb up the trunks of coconut palms by gripping with its powerful pincers. It strips off the coconuts so they fall to the ground, ready for the crab to eat.

These tree-climbing crustaceans live on the tropical islands in the Pacific and Indian Oceans, and are about 45cm (18in) long.

How old are dolls?

Dolls have been around since there were children! At first they were very simple - just a piece of cloth with a crudely drawn face or a piece of carved wood or bone.

The Egyptians had dolls with movable limbs. In Roman times children played with rag dolls.

Greek clay dolls had cords attached to their arms and legs, so they moved up and down when pulled. The Romans had dolls' furniture made of lead, so they may have had dolls' houses too!

Up to the 19th century dolls were made of cloth and leather, often with hand-carved heads. In Europe, after the 1850s, dolls' faces were made with wax; heads and trunks of papier mache and cloth bodies stuffed with sawdust, which often trickled out!

The more expensive dolls had beautiful faces with heads and hands made of porcelain. They had long hair and glass eyes and were sometimes dressed in Paris fashions.

Who made dolls talk?

Two famous inventors gave dolls speaking voices. In 1827 Johann Maelzel, the German inventor of the metronome, put a voice box into a doll. When you gave it a squeeze, it said 'Mamma' and 'Papa'.

Later in the 1880s, Thomas Edison, the inventor of the phonograph or gramophone, designed a specially made phonographic cylinder small enough to fit inside a doll. A nursery rhyme was recorded on the tiny cylinder for the doll to recite.

Where is the world's longest wall?

The Great Wall of China is 2,400km (1,500 miles) long, 7m (23ft) high, and a roadway of 5.5m (18ft) runs along the top.

It was thought that this would be the only structure that would be visible from the Moon. We now know that nothing man-made can be seen at that distance.

Who built the Great Wall of China?

The first Chinese emperor is usually given credit for building the wall around 215BC. In fact, large parts of the wall were already 200 years old. Shi Huangdi ordered the sections to be joined together to keep out the wild Mongol tribes from the north. Hundreds of thousands of soldiers, slaves and criminals worked and died on the wall.

The Great Wall did not stop the Mongol army of Genghis Khan in the 13th century from invading China.

Who was buried with an army?

It was the same man, emperor Shi Huangdi. In 1974 workers digging a well near the tomb of the emperor found a life-size terracotta soldier. So began one of the world's greatest ever archaeological finds.

So far, 6,000 warriors, horses and chariots have been found. All are made in terracotta - originally they had been painted to look real, and were fully armed with real weapons.

What is terracotta?

It is clay baked to a brownish red, but not glazed. The name means 'baked earth'.

Who else built a great wall?

The Romans invaded Britain in AD43. Within 40 years the whole country was under Roman rule. The wild tribes of the north caused many problems, so the emperor Hadrian built a great wall in AD120-130. It passed through present day Newcastle and on past Carlisle to the west coast.

It had forts and watchtowers every mile along its 120km (75 mile) length. It was the most northern part of the Roman Empire. Parts of the wall can still be seen today.

What was the Roman army like?

The Roman Empire became the most powerful in the world because it had the best army in the world for hundreds of years.

Each man was well trained and equipped and fought in a well organised unit. Their enemies were mostly wild tribesmen who could not match the Roman fighting skill and discipline. The Romans were also skilled at building forts and bridges, so nothing could stop their advance.

A 'mile' castle, these were spread out along the length of the wall

What was a centurion?

The Roman army fought in units of 100 men (a century). Their commander was called a centurion.

Did you know the Romans used catapults?

They were large machines that could throw a stone as heavy as a man. Other types called ballista were big like crossbows.

Do you believe in Roman ghosts?

One of the strangest sightings of ghosts happened in the historic city of York in England.

A plumber was working alone in the cellar of an old building when he heard the blast of a trumpet. A Roman soldier on horseback came through the wall followed by a whole column of armed soldiers. The strangest thing was that the lower parts of the soldiers' legs were below floor level.

It was later found that the original Roman road was 50cm (20in) below the cellar floor!

Did Nero fiddle while Rome burned?

No! In AD64, a great midday fire destroyed two thirds of Rome while Nero was away at the seaside. He couldn't have played the fiddle either - it wasn't invented until the 16th century!

How many penguins live in the Arctic?

Penguins live in the South Pole - there are none in the Arctic at all!

Were the bagpipes invented in Scotland?

Romans played bagpipes in the first century and they were used in the Middle East, Persia and Arabia centuries ago. King Henry VIII had a set of his own, and folk tunes of Ireland, France, Spain, Italy, Russia, Scandinavia and, of course, Scotland, are often accompanied by the bagpipes.

What is Big Ben?

Big Ben is the bell that chimes the hours in the clock tower of the Houses of Parliament. It is not the clock itself! Installed in 1859, Big Ben rings out the hours after the Westminster chimes.

What is a coracle?

A wickerwork boat like a round canoe, covered in skins and made watertight with a covering of tar. Coracles were in use in pre-Roman times and they are still used in Wales today.

What does 'dead as a dodo' mean?

This phrase means totally dead - extinct! The dodo was discovered in Mauritius in 1507 and was extinct by 1681. This big bird with short wings could not fly to escape its enemies.

What is a Portuguese man-of-war?

It sounds like a galleon, but it is really a very dangerous type of jellyfish! Its poisonous stinging tentacles up to 25m (82ft) long can sometimes kill humans.

Was the yo-yo invented in America?

The toy came into the USA in the 1920s from the Philippines where the word 'yo-yo' means 'come come'. In the Orient and ancient Greece yo-yos had been popular for centuries.

How did the teddy bear get its name?

President Theodore Roosevelt was out hunting in Mississippi in 1902 when he refused to shoot a bear cub. The story was reported in the newspapers and after that the first toy bears were made, known as Teddy's bear.

What is a figurehead?

In the old days of wooden sailing ships, the builders would add a carved figurehead, often of a woman, on the bow as a ship's mascot. They were usually brightly painted.

Who was America's first president?

George Washington became America's first president on April 30 1779. He was a plantation owner, soldier and president for eight years. You can still visit his estate at Mount Vernon, Virginia.

Did he really chop down that cherry tree?

When George Washington's father asked his son if he had really chopped down his cherry tree, young George replied, "I cannot tell a lie!" Then he confessed. This story was made up years later by his biographer.

What was the Kon Tiki?

The Norwegian explorer Thor Heyerdahl built a raft of balsa logs - the Kon Tiki. In 1947, together with a crew of five, he crossed 6,900km (4,300 miles) of open ocean from Callao in Peru to a coral reef east of Tahiti.

It took 101 days, but he proved that Incas could have made the same journey 1,500 years ago.

What is a magnet?

It is a piece of metal that can attract or repel other metals. The ends of a magnet are opposite poles. One end will point to the North Pole, the other to the South Pole, this is how a compass needle works. If you put two magnets togther, North Pole to North Pole they push apart.

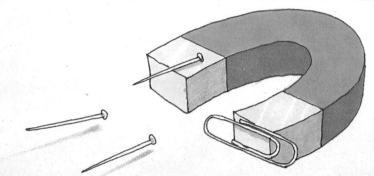

Why do hurricanes have names?

Because of an Australian weatherman called Clement Wet Wragge. When he quarrelled with someone, he named the next hurricane after them.

Now each year a list is drawn up of girls' and boys' names in alphabetical order, ready for future hurricanes.

What is a fjord?

Fjords are long, deep inlets from the sea, found in the glacial valleys of Norway.

During the ice age, glaciers cut these valleys, and when the ice finally melted, sea water flooded in.

What is a silhouette?

There was once a French statesman well known in the 1700s for doing things as economically as possible - his name was Etienne Silhouette. He gave his name to those simple black shadow portraits.

Who wrote Frankenstein?

Late one night on the shores of Lake Geneva, Lord Byron suggested his friends wrote ghost stories. So Mary Shelley, wife of poet Percy Bysshe Shelley, created the frightening monster Frankenstein - she was just 19.

Where does silk come from?

Silk is a fine thread produced by silk worms. A silk worm lays eggs on a mulberry leaf, which the caterpillar eats when it emerges. After a month they spin a silk cocoon around themselves. Before they can develop into a silk moth, the cocoons are taken and soaked in hot water to make silk and the pupa dies. One silk worm can spin up to 1.2km (3,900ft) of single thread.

What is the United Nations?

It is an association of nations set up in 1945, to help poor countries improve living conditions, to promote peace and international cooperation, and to uphold the rights of people of all races and religions.

The UN government headquarters (opened in 1952) is in New York, built on land given by John D. Rockefeller.

What is UNICEF?

It is the United Nations Children's Fund, founded in 1946 to help the children of the world. In 1965 the fund won the Nobel Prize for peace.

Who lives on a sampan?

Many Chinese live all their lives on floating, flat-bottomed wooden boats called sampans.

In some cities where space is limited, people live crowded together on sampans in big harbours. Some boats sell goods, others are used for fishing by day, and sleeping on by night.

Which insect can walk on water?

Many pond insects seem to walk on water. They do so because of the surface tension. The pond skater's legs press into a kind of elastic skin on the surface of the water - but don't go through!

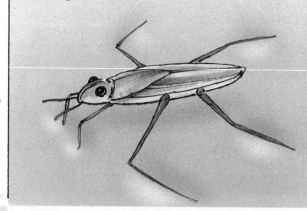

What is a sedan chair?

In the 18th century, wealthy people hired sedan chairs. They were carried through the dirty streets by two strong chairmen and this protected their fine clothes and elaborate hairstyles.

Where is the world's tallest structure?

The CN Tower in Toronto, Canada. This self supporting tower is 553m (1,814ft) high. It has a revolving restaurant at 347m (1,140ft). As you eat, you can see the hills 120km (75 miles) away.

Can you really hear the sea in a seashell?

You are hearing ordinary sounds echoing and re-echoing as the air inside the shell vibrates. Another roaring sound is the amplified sound of the blood rushing through your own ear!

Is the white rhino really white?

No - it is the same colour as the black rhino! It has a wide upper lip and grazes like a cow. The black rhino's lip is pointed for plucking twigs and leaves.

Why do opossums play dead?

The expression 'playing possum' means pretending to be dead. Opossums do this when trying to escape the attention of an enemy or facing danger.

Who was Queen Boadicea?

The Queen of an ancient British tribe, the Iceni. She led her followers in fierce and bloody battles against the Romans. In AD62 she was defeated and poisoned herself.

Who painted themselves with woad?

The ancient Britons dyed their bodies with woad, a blue dye made from the leaves of the woad plant. Their painted blue tattoos made them more fearsome in battle.

Where is the world's highest lake?

Lake Titicaca 3,810m (12,500ft) high up in the Andes. It is the longest lake in South America 190km (118 miles) long. The local Indians made reed boats from the reed forests by the lake.

What is the Statue of Liberty?

This is the huge and beautiful statue that stands on Liberty Island in New York harbour. She was made in France and given as a gift to America by the people of France.

How tall is she?

The figure stands at 46m (151ft) tall, but she stands on a pedestal of the same height, making her 92m (302ft) tall altogether.

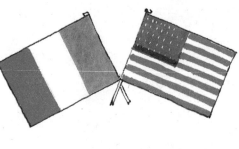

Who built her?

The idea for the statue came from Edouard de Laboulaye, a French professor in 1865. He discussed it with his friend the sculptor Frederic Auguste Bartholdi, who later designed and built the huge figure which he called Liberty Enlightening the World.

It was 21 years later that the statue was completed in 1886.

Why is she green?

The figure is made of thin copper sheets beaten into shape over a frame. When copper is exposed to the weather it turns pale green.

Does her torch light up?

The original torch was lit from inside, but the light was very poor. Liberty was given her second torch earlier this century, but over the years it was damaged by rain.

In 1984 she was given a new torch covered in gold leaf. With spotlights on the outside it looks as if the torch is alight.

Where is there another statue just like her?

There is a smaller copy of the statue by the River Seine in Paris, which is where she was designed and built.

How tall is the Eiffel Tower?

This famous tower, which must be one of the wonders of the modern world, stands 300m (984ft) high and dominates the Paris skyline.

How heavy is it?

It weighs 7,100 tonnes, which is not very heavy for something so gigantic.

What was it used for?

It was built for the 1889 Paris exhibition as a rival to the Crystal Palace in London. It was only expected to last for 20 years, but it was so useful as a telegraph station, and later as a radio mast, that it still stands today.

What is the link between the tower and the Statue of Liberty?

The answer is the man who designed the tower, Gustav Eiffel. The statue in New York is made of thin copper sheets, but the huge size is supported by an iron frame inside. This was designed and built by the French engineer Eiffel some years before his famous tower. He became known as the magician of iron.

What famous cathedral is on an island in Paris?

The national church of France, Notre Dame, stands on the Ile de la Cité in the River Seine.

Did you know that the Louvre was once a royal palace?

Today the Louvre is the home of some of the world's greatest art treasures, holding 200,000 exhibits, but it was once the residence of the Kings of France.

Who built the Arc de Triomphe?

The building of this huge gateway was ordered by Napoleon in 1806. Beautifully decorated with sculptures, it took 30 years to complete.

Is there really a seahorse?

This small saltwater fish 4-30cm (1.5-12in) long looks like a tiny hobby horse.

It has a prehensile tail (it can grasp things) and it swims upright.

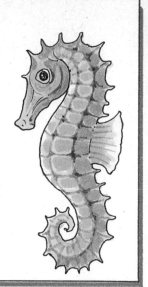

What is astrology?

There is a belief that events can be foretold by studying the position of the planets and stars in the sky when someone was born.

Astrologers refer to this part of the sky as the zodiac. The constellations of the zodiac are divided into 12 groups, each with its own sign.

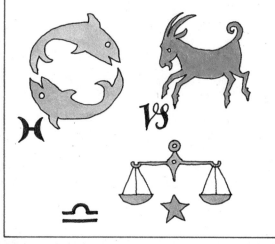

Where does the Red Cross symbol come from?

The symbol is a red cross on a white background, the reverse of the national flag of Switzerland.

In 1864 a young Swiss businessman, Henri Dunant, formed the International Red Cross, for the relief of suffering in war.

Nowadays, the Red Cross also provide relief in natural disasters such as earthquakes, floods and hurricanes.

Swiss flag

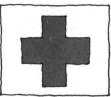

Red Cross flag

Which two countries play cricket for the ashes?

In test matches between England and Australia, the two teams play for the ashes, which is an urn containing the ashes of a burned stump.

The urn is kept at Lord's cricket ground, London - even when Australia wins a test series against England!

What is astronomy?

A science about the movement, distances and sizes of the Sun, Moon, stars, planets, meteors, constellations and comets within our and other solar systems.

Thousands of years ago some groups of stars were given names, because their shape was similar to a bear, a dog, a lion or perhaps a plough!

How useful is this tree?

Lots of products come from the coco palm tree. Boats are made from the trunk; leaves are used for thatching, basket making, mats and hats; coir fibre from the husks is used for ropes and matting. The coconut oil, milk and leaf buds are all edible products that come from this tree.

What are molluscs?

Molluscs are a major group of animals that include shellfish, snails and slugs. They have soft, limbless bodies with no skeleton - most of them are protected by a hard shell. Squids, octopuses and cuttlefish have internal skeletons.

Most molluscs live in the sea, but some live in fresh water or on land. They are cold blooded.

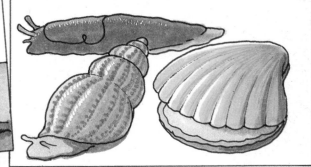

Is the croissant French?

In 1683 Vienna was under siege from the Turks. Men baking bread during the night heard the Turkish army tunnelling under the city. They raised the alarm, saved the city and baked croissants in the shape of the crescent Moon on the Turkish flag!

What was the Phoenix?

It was a fabulous bird of Egyptian myth. It lived for 500 years, built a nest of spices and burned itself to ashes. From the ashes came a young bird that lived for the next 500 years.

Where is the land of the Midnight Sun?

Lapland is a region mainly inside the Arctic circle. It stretches across the north of Norway, Sweden and Finland.

This is the land of the Midnight Sun, which shines continually for 24 hours a day, for 73 days from mid-May to the end of July.

Where did American Indians come from?

Until 20-30,000 years ago there were no human beings on the continent of America. The Indians are the descendants of Mongoloid people who crossed from Asia into Canada and slowly travelled all the way down to South America.

Why are they called Indians?

When Christopher Columbus arrived in America in 1492 he thought he had reached India! So he named the native inhabitants Indians and the name has remained.

What is a tepee?

The tepee is a large tent made of skins that the plains Indians lived in. Supported on long poles, they could easily be moved. The Indians of the south, such as the Apache, lived in a framework covered in branches, reeds or skins. They called this a wickiup.

Who were the medicine men?

They were the doctors of the tribe, but their main purpose was to deal with the spirits which the Indians believed were all around.

What was a peace pipe?

The peace pipe was a sacred object to the Indians. Called a 'calumet' it was usually made out of stone. All important dealings were sealed with the smoking of the peace pipe. To break your word after this would make the spirits very angry.

What was a tomahawk?

This was a light war axe. Until white people introduced iron, tomahawks were made of chipped stone tied to a handle.

Did the Indians always have horses?

Horses did not exist in America until the Spaniards brought them in the 16th century. It was over 100 years before the Indians had them. At first the Indians were terrified of the horse, but later they became the best horsemen in the world.

Do you know what moccasins are?

These were the shoes made by the women of the tribe. The tops were made of soft leather, often decorated with beads or dyes. The soles were of tough buffalo hide. They were stitched together with animal sinews.

How did Indian mothers carry their babies?

Babies were strapped to wooden cradle boards. They were highly decorated and were carried on the mother's back.

How did Indian families travel?

The Indians did not have the wheel. When they had to move, they made a sledge from two tepee poles drawn by a horse or even a dog. The sledge was called a 'travois'. As well as their possessions, elderly members of the family would travel this way.

Who first trained guide dogs for the blind?

During the First World War, a doctor at a German hospital left his German shepherd dog to look after a patient for a few minutes.

The way the dog behaved impressed the doctor so much that he began training dogs purely to help the blind.

Which tree can you hold in your hand?

Bonsai is the art of arranging and growing trees in miniature. The Japanese word 'bonsai' means 'they planted'!

With careful pruning over many years, these dwarf trees look exactly like a fully grown tree. Some are hundreds of years old and very valuable.

What is the spectrum?

Without light there is no colour. Sunlight seems to be white light, but it is made up of seven colours: red, orange, yellow, green, blue, indigo and violet. When sunlight passes through a prism it spreads out into a rainbow band of these colours, called the spectrum.

When sunlight shines through rain it is split up by the droplets into a rainbow.

Where is El Dorado?

A legendary city of gold supposed to exist in South America. A Spaniard thought he glimpsed a vast city roofed with gold, and since the 16th century many explorers have gone in search of 'the golden'!

Who was St Christopher?

In order to serve God, St Christopher carried travellers across a fast-flowing river.

One day as he was carrying a little child, he felt he had the sins of the whole world on his shoulders. It was the infant Christ as all the pictures of St Christopher now show!

What is karate?

The word means 'empty hands', fighting without weapons. Karate is a fast dangerous fighting sport using punches, kicks and throws. Originally from China, karate has been developed in Japan where the first school (dojo) was set up in 1924.

Karate can be used for self-defence or attack.

What is judo?

Judo was probably developed by Chinese Buddhist monks to defend themselves without hurting their attacker. By using holds, throws and falls the attacker's size can be used against them.

There are no punches or kicks used in judo, it is mainly used for self defence.

What was Pegasus?

In Greek mythology Pegasus was a fabulous winged horse, which sprang from the blood of Medusa, after Perseus had cut off her head.

Pegasus flew to heaven and a constellation is named after him.

How does a nettle sting?

The leaves and stem of a nettle are covered in microscopic sharp pointed hairs. A stinging fluid passes through these hairs and the flesh of anyone touching the nettle.

What do 'port' and 'starboard' mean?

In the days before boats had a central rudder they were steered by an oar called a 'steer board' on the right hand side.

To avoid crushing the steer board, the boat tied up in port on the left hand side, hence the names 'port' and 'starboard'.

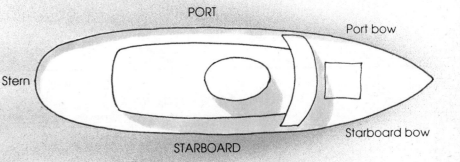

PORT

Port bow

Stern

Starboard bow

STARBOARD

What time is it?

Almost everything in our lives is controlled by time. Time to get up! Time to catch the bus! Time to go to school! We have clocks and watches that tell us the exact time to the second. But how did people tell the time in the past?

How do you tell the time with a stick?

Early humans noticed that as the Sun passed overhead during the day, shadows moved around. By placing a row of evenly spaced stones in front of a stick, the moving shadow measured the time passing.

What is a water clock?

The ancient Egyptians measured time by water dripping from a marked jar. The Greeks dripped water into a jar which made a float rise and turn the hand of a clock.

What is a sundial?

The sundial works just like the stick and the stones. People put them in their gardens or on buildings and tell the time by the moving shadow. The trouble was they didn't work in the dark!

Can you tell the time by candlelight?

Candles were once used to measure time. If you cut evenly spaced notches in the candle, as it burns down it gives a rough idea of the time.

Can you measure time with sand?

The hour glass was a good way of measuring time. It was in use for hundreds of years. Fine sand trickles through a small hole in the glass from the top half to the bottom. When the top is empty the glass is turned over. Tournaments were timed by the turn of a glass.

What is money?

Money, in the form of coins, notes or plastic cards, has a known value and can be exchanged for goods of an equal value.

The ancient Egyptians used gold and silver by weight. They would carry bits of silver wire or lumps of gold and cut pieces off. Other people had even stranger money.

Who had the largest money?

The people of Yap, an island in the Pacific Ocean, carved stone discs as money. Some were up to 4m (12ft) wide.

Who could eat their money?

In Africa salt is valuable, so bars of rock salt wrapped in reeds were used as money. Goods can also be bought with cattle or goats.

Who would pay with seashells?

Small cowrie shells were used as money in many parts of the world. They were known to be used in ancient China and in parts of Africa up to the last century.

Who made their money with beads?

The North American Indians made belts of beads called 'wampum'. These belts, like the stones of Yap were used to settle agreements between villages or tribes, they were not really for buying goods.

Who paid in axe heads or knives?

The ancient Chinese used tools for trade and their earliest coins were shaped like knives and hoes. These were difficult to carry and were replaced by round coins. Money axes were also used in Mexico. Made of copper, they were too soft to be real tools.

Who started the use of paper money?

In the 10th century the Chinese coins were made of iron and very heavy. People began leaving their money with merchants who would give them a written receipt for its value. The idea of paper money grew from this.

Where did the first Olympic Games take place?

These ancient games were part of a religious event, sacred to the god Zeus. They were held every four years on the plain of Olympia, at the foot of Mount Kronos in southern Greece.

Were the games held in special buildings?

On the site at Olympia was a great temple and altar to Zeus. Athletic events were held in the stadium, and races for horses and chariots took place in the Hippodrome. There was a wrestling ground by the river, a gymnasium and baths. Ruins of the site can still be seen today.

How many years did the ancient Olympics last?

The games lasted for almost 1,200 years from 776 BC until AD 393, when the Christian emperor of Rome, Theodosius I, abolished them. He said the games were pagan!

Which five events make up the ancient pentathlon?

Running, jumping, discus, javelin and wrestling.

What happened to Olympia?

Most of the buildings collapsed during an earthquake 1,000 years after they were built.

How did the ancient competitors dress?

They didn't! Ancient athletes wore no clothes at all when they competed in the events.

Did the Grecian women break any records?

None at all! Women were barred from competing in the games. Young girls were allowed in as spectators, but wives could be put to death for watching or taking part.

All competitors had to be male, of Greek descent and Greek speakers.

How did the marathon get its name?

Marathon was a town in ancient Greece. In 490BC a great battle was held there between the Greeks and the Persians. News of the Greek victory was taken 26 miles to Athens by a runner named Pheidippides, who fell dead from exhaustion as he entered the city.

The marathon commemorates his amazing run.

Which film star won five Olympic medals?

Johnny Weissmuller, who played Tarzan, won five gold medals for swimming in the 1924 and 1928 games.

How long is a modern marathon?

In the London games of 1908 officials added 385 yards to the 26 mile race. That meant the race would end exactly in front of the royal box, and King Edward VII would have a good view.

From then on the official marathon distance became 26 miles, 385 yards (42.195m).

When was the first women's marathon?

Women were not allowed to run an Olympic marathon until 1984.

When were the first winter Olympics?

They took place in 1924 on snow and ice in the French Alps at Chamonix, in the shadow of Mont Blanc.

Why does the Olympic flag have five rings?

Five interlaced rings on a white background represent the five inhabited continents: Africa, America, Asia, Australasia and Europe. The five different colours of the rings are decorative.

Are Olympic medals pure gold?

No! Olympic medals are made of gilded silver.

When did the modern Olympics begin?

They were revived in 1896. A Frenchman, Baron Pierre de Coubertin first had the idea, which he put before an International Congress of 15 nations in Paris. They agreed that the Olympic Games should begin once more and be held every four years.

Where did they hold the first modern games?

Appropriately, they were held in Athens. King George I of Greece opened the very first modern Olympic Games.

How many times have the games been cancelled?

During the two World Wars the games could not take place in 1916, 1940 and 1944.

Which five events make up the modern pentathlon?

Running, swimming, fencing, shooting and horse riding.

Who were pirates?

They were sea-robbers who attacked and stole from other ships and travellers on the high seas.

Piracy has gone on since people first sailed the sea. Ships of ancient Greece and Rome were often attacked crossing the Mediterranean. Vikings (the word means 'pirates') used to raid the coasts of Britain and Western Europe. During the seventeenth and eighteenth centuries pirates hunted and plundered ships across the seven seas.

Who was Blackbeard?

His real name was Edward Teach, but the name Blackbeard once struck terror into the hearts of anyone who sailed the seas.

His name came from his black waist-length beard tied up with ribbons. This fearsome man stuck slow-burning tapers under his hat, six pistols in his belt and a cutlass in his hand before swarming over the side of an enemy ship.

Who were the buccaneers?

They were sailors who had deserted their ships, escaped slaves, runaway servants, and men from different countries, and they all gathered on the island of Hispaniola (today known as Haiti and the Dominican Republic). These men hunted the wild cattle of the area, which they killed for food. They hung thin strips of the meat to dry over special wire frames called 'boucaniers' or buccaneers. Around 1630 the buccaneers began to attack the Spanish treasure ships that passed their island shores. At first they used dug-out canoes. Later they built flat-bottomed sailing ships that could lie in wait in the shallow waters around the coasts of the Spanish Main.

How did Blackbeard die?

He was killed in 1718 after boarding Lieutenant Maynard's Royal Navy sloop. Blackbeard died after receiving five bullet wounds and 20 gashes from a cutlass.

Where was the Spanish Main?

The southern coasts of North America and the islands of the West Indies in the Caribbean were known as the Spanish Main.

Spanish galleons heavily laden with gold plundered from the New World often set sail for Spain, some were attacked by pirates and never reached home!

GULF OF MEXICO

SPANISH MAIN

What are 'pieces of eight'?

Spanish pieces of eight were silver coins worth eight reales. They were shipped in huge quantities between Europe and Mexico by the powerful Spanish empire. Commonly known as dollars, they and the gold doubloon coin were the main targets of pirates.

What flag did the pirates fly?

No one knows for certain whether pirates really did hoist the Jolly Roger. It is thought that most pirate ships flew a simple black flag and not the skull and crossbones!

Who wrote a novel about a pirate's buried treasure?

Robert Louis Stevenson wrote *Treasure Island*, which tells how a group of friends go in search of a pirate's treasure. They are betrayed by their own crew, who are really pirates headed by the notorious Long John Silver.

Who was the pirate captain in Peter Pan?

The blackest rogue of all - Captain Hook! He had a mean scowling face with dark eyes that glowed when he used his hook, for Peter Pan had chopped off his hand and thrown it to a passing crocodile.

Did pirates make you walk the plank?

Although pirate captains could be very cruel - often torturing and killing their victims - making you walk the plank seems to be a myth!

What are truffles?

Truffles are an expensive food delicacy used in the very best French patés. They look like large spongy walnuts and grow in the ground. Because they like to eat them, pigs are often used to find truffles.

What was tulipmania?

Although still one of the world's favourite flowers, when it was introduced into Europe 400 years ago the tulip caused 'tulipmania'. Rare bulbs were worth as much as a house, particularly in Holland.

What is the difference between rabbits and hares?

The hare is often mistaken for its cousin, the rabbit, yet it is very different. Hares are larger with longer legs, they do not live underground like the rabbit and are immune to the disease myxomatosis that kills many rabbits.

What are baby hares called?

They are called leverets and are born with a full coat of fur.

What is a Tasmanian devil?

This fierce animal used to live in Australia, but is now only found in Tasmania. About 1m (40in) long from nose to tail, it only comes out at night. It feeds on small animals, birds, lizards and even wallabies if it can catch them.

What makes bread rise?

Bread dough is made to rise by the reproduction of minute fungus cells of yeast. Add yeast to a sugar solution and it multiplies rapidly. When flour is kneaded with yeast, water and salt, the yeast generates bubbles of carbon dioxide and makes the dough rise, which retains its shape when baked in the hot oven.

Was Sir Isaac Newton really hit on the head by an apple?

The story of this great English scientist discovering the law of gravity by being hit on the head is not true, although it *was* an apple that started him thinking about gravity that led to great developments in science and the study of astronomy.

He also invented a reflecting telescope and it was Newton who first realised what causes a glass prism to split light into the colour of the rainbow, the spectrum.

The apple tree which started it all was blown down in 1820.

Who cooked an omelette while on a tightrope?

The great tightrope walker Blondin performed many daring feats, but one of his strangest was in 1862 at London's Crystal Palace. He carried a 23kg (50lb) stove out to the middle of the rope. After lighting it, he cooked an omelette, still balancing himself and the stove high above the crowd.

What is Stonehenge?

Standing on Salisbury Plain is the greatest relic of prehistoric times to be found in Britain. It is a circle of huge stones, which look like doorways. No one knows who built it or why. It was probably built around 1700BC and may have been a temple for Sun worship. Centuries later it was used by the Celtic druids for their ceremonies.

Who was the first Santa Claus?

Many people believe it was Saint Nicholas. He was the bishop of Myra in Asia Minor back in the fourth century.

One day this kind old man heard of a merchant who was too poor to give his three daughters money to be married. So St Nicholas dropped three bags of gold down the chimney of their house. Next morning the three girls found the bags of gold in their stockings, which they had hung up the night before.

That is why children in some countries hang up stockings hoping that Santa Claus will fill them with gifts.

St Nicholas became the patron saint of children, and his feast day is on December 6th.

What happens on St Nicholas's Day?

In some countries it is a children's holiday and St Nicholas brings his gifts on December 6th, three weeks before Christmas. Other countries look forward to the visit of Santa Claus on Christmas Eve, but some lucky children receive gifts on both days!

How does St Nicholas arrive in Holland?

On St Nicholas Eve, December 5th, a boat sails into Amsterdam carrying St Nicholas and his servant Black Peter. Good children get presents, but Black Peter chases the bad ones with his stick!

Santa Claus comes from Sankt Klaus, which was the Dutch name for St Nicholas.

Who leaves shoes by the fireside?

On Christmas Eve in France, children put their shoes by the fireside to be filled with presents by Père Noel or Father Christmas. In some parts of France they keep a yule log burning for all the 12 days of Christmas.

What happened to St Lucia?

Christmas in Sweden begins on December 13, which is St Lucia's day.

Long ago the early Christians were persecuted and had to meet in dark underground caves. St Lucia risked her life to bring them food. On her head she wore a crown of candles to light her way. One day she was caught by the Roman Emperor's soldiers and killed.

Today she is remembered each Christmas by young Swedish girls. They get up early on St Lucia's day, dress as she did to take buns and coffee to their families - who are still in bed!

What does the word Advent mean?

Christians all over the world celebrate Advent during the four weeks before Christmas. Advent means 'arrival' or 'coming', and people prepare for the coming of Christ on Christmas Eve.

What is an Advent calendar?

In Germany children look forward to opening the 24 numbered doors on this special calendar. Just one door is opened each day to find a small Christmas picture inside. The last one is opened on Christmas Eve.

Who hits a Pinata?

In Mexico all through the Christmas festival, children have great fun when they are blind-folded and hit a pinata with a stick. The hollow clay pinata jars are hung above the children's heads. They hit them with sticks, and when at last the jar splits, sweets and treats spill all over the floor!

Who are Julnissen?

In Scandinavian countries these are little elves who live under the floorboards and in barns. They look after the family and the animals.

On Christmas Eve, if a bowl of porridge is left out for these little fellows, they will come out and hide presents all round the house. If the porridge is forgotten, the Julnissen will play tricks on the family all the next year!

Who is Befana?

In Italy children wait for the good witch Befana. She rides over the rooftops astride her broomstick on Epiphany Eve or Twelfth Night.

She drops gifts for the good children down the chimney, and a piece of coal for the naughty ones!

What is the Epiphany?

This is a Christian festival celebrated on January 6th, when the Three Kings arrived in Bethlehem to bring their gifts to the Christ child.

What about the reindeer?

In America, England and many other countries, Father Christmas or Santa Claus has become the symbol of Christmas for children.

With his white beard and red cloak, carrying a sackful of presents over his shoulder, he travels from the North Pole on his sleigh pulled by reindeer. On Christmas Eve he rides over the rooftops and climbs down the chimneys with gifts for well-behaved boys and girls.

What is the largest state in the USA?
Alaska! 1,478,425 sq. km (570,823 sq. miles). Twice the size of Texas, the next largest.

What was the first antibiotic?
Penicillin was discovered by accident by Alexander Fleming in 1928. Returning from a month's holiday, he found that mould growing on a culture plate had killed some of the harmful bacteria. The first antibiotic was named after the mould!

What was first on the Moon?
On September 14 1959, the Soviet Lunik II space craft crashed onto the Moon. It was the first man-made object to reach the Moon.

Where did golf begin?
It began in Scotland and was first mentioned in 1497 when King James II banned the sport. Men were spending too much time playing golf instead of weapon practice in case of war.

What is a cookie cutter?
A small shark, only 50cm (20in) long, which bites cookie-sized pieces out of dolphins, whales and rubber dinghies.

How many ants does an anteater eat?
The anteater tears the ants' nest apart with its powerful claws. Then he shoots out his long sticky, worm-like tongue and eats about 30,000 ants a day!

What is your pulse rate?
The average pulse rate of an adult male is 70-72 beats per minute. For a female the average is 78-82.

Which dog is named after a state?
The tiny Chihuahua dog was named after the state in Mexico. It is the smallest breed of dog, sometimes called 'ornament' or 'pillow' dog.

Which of the Seven Wonders Of The World still survives?
From ancient times only one can be seen and visited today - the Pyramids of Egypt.

What is Esperanto?
An international language created by Ludovic Zamenhof in 1887. It is a phonetic language, easy for people of many countries to learn and understand.

Who took the first photograph?
In 1826 Niceephore Niepce took the very first photograph. It was of his barnyard in France. Dr Edwin Land's Polaroid camera took the first 'instant' snaps in 1944.

How old is basketball?
In 1891 Professor James Naismith of the YMCA College in Springfield, Massachusetts thought of a game that could be played in a gymnasium. Basketball has been popular ever since.

When was margarine first eaten?
It was first made in France in 1870. The country was at war and butter was scarce. Napoleon III offered a reward for a substitute.

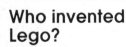

Who invented Lego?
Lego comes from the Danish words 'leg godt' which means to play well. Lego bricks were designed by the Dane Ole Kirk Christiansen in 1955.

Who made the first parachute jump?

Sitting inside a tiny basket, Frenchman André Garnerin, parachuted from a hot-air balloon as it floated above Paris in 1797.

Did spinach make Popeye strong?

In the 1890s nutrition experts put a decimal point in the wrong place and said that it contained ten times more iron then it did. It has no more iron for strength than any other greens!

Who was the human fly?

American George Willig climbed up the sheer face of tall buildings like a fly. In 1977 he climbed the outside of the 110 storey World Trade Centre, New York.

Who were the Pharaohs?

Ancient Egypt was ruled by a Pharaoh - a dynasty or family of kings. There were 31 dynasties, beginning in 4,400BC. The Pharaohs ruled Egypt for about 4,000 years.

Are canaries from the Canary Islands?

These brightly coloured singing birds are named after the islands, one of which was called by the Romans Canaria Insula or Isle of Dogs. Large dogs lived there and the Latin word for 'dog' is 'canis'.

Which film star broke a record?

When Johnny Weissmuller (Tarzan) was 18, he became the first man to swim 100 metres (328 ft) in less than a minute.

What is a pygmy?

Pygmies are races or groups of people who are less than 1.5m (59in) tall. The bushmen of the Kalahari desert and the Bambuti of the African Congo are pygmies.

Can fish climb trees?

The American mudskipper can as it goes in search of insects. They breathe air through their gills and use their front fins as feet.

Where can you find black swans?

They are native to Australia and live round the coasts and in the lakes. Only the tips of their wings are white.

Who invented the first vacuum cleaner?

When Londoner Henry Booth designed the first vacuum cleaner in 1921 he formed a company that would clean your house using his new invention.

What is a monkey puzzle?

The monkey puzzle tree or Chile pine with its branches covered in sharp scaly leaves is the only tree that a monkey cannot climb! It was brought from South America to Europe in 1796.

What makes waves?

Wind, earthquakes, explosions caused by underwater volcanoes, all make waves. Tides are caused by the pull of the Sun and the Moon.

Who was Jupiter?

Chief god of the Romans, his Greek name was Zeus. He had power over rain, tempest, thunder and lightning.

Who eats locust bread?

The Arabs dry locusts in the sun, pound them into a powder and bake them into bread. Sometimes they are fried in butter.

Which dancer named a cake?

The Russian ballerina, Anna Pavlova, had a delicious fruit-filled meringue cake named after her while on a tour of Australia.

Where is the largest amount of gold in the world?

There are 12,500 tonnes stored in the vaults of the Federal Reserve Bank of New York.

Who gave his name to America?

Although Amerigo Vespucci did not discover America, he described his voyages there so vividly that the new continent was named after him.